£12·To

Exploring the Past through Place-Names:
Woolverstone

OTHER BOOKS ON PLACE-NAMES
FROM 'PAUL WATKINS'

Richard Coates, *The Ancient and Modern Names of the Channel Islands. A Linguistic History*

Joyce Miles, *A Dictionary of House Names* (forthcoming)

W. F. H. Nicolaisen, *Collected Essays on Scottish Place-Names* (provisional title, forthcoming)

Adrian Room, *The Street Names of England*

Alex Rumble and A. D. Mills (eds), *Names, Places and People: an Onomastic Miscellany in Memory of John McNeal Dodgson* (forthcoming)

Jeffrey Spittal and John Field, *A Reader's Guide to the Place-Names of the United Kingdom. A Bibliography of Publications (1920-1989) on the Place-Names of Great Britain and Northern Ireland, the Isle of Man and the Channel Islands.* An updated *Supplement* to this is forthcoming

Finally, Paul Watkins is also the distributor of *Nomina*, the journal of the Society for Names Studies of Britain and Ireland. Volumes 1 to 16 are all available and 'Paul Watkins' has recently produced a catalogue of the journal's contents. A catalogue of our medieval history titles is also available.

EXPLORING THE PAST
THROUGH PLACE-NAMES:
WOOLVERSTONE

Sylvia Laverton

PAUL WATKINS

STAMFORD

Published by
PAUL WATKINS
18, Adelaide Street
Stamford, Lincolnshire
PE9 2EN

ISBN

1 871615 78 X

printed on long-life paper

Printed by Woolnoughs of Irthlingborough

CONTENTS

List of illustrations   vii

Acknowledgements   ix

Foreword by Gwen Dyke   x

Introduction   xi

I. From Wolverston Manor to present-day Woolverstone: 1300-1990   1
   Origins of manor and estate   1
   The Berners' architectural legacy   3
   The post-Berners years   5

II. Woolverstone Parish: 1840-1990   10
   Tithe Map and present place-names   11

III. Wolverston to Woolverstone: place-names 1300-1840   19
   Alphabetical List with Notes on Sources   20
   Appendix: Place-Names in Date Order 1348-1635   47

IV. A 'map' of the Manor: 1350-1600   54

V. Roads and tracks   56
   The oldest ways   56
   Ways to Pin Mill   58
   Tileyard and mill   58
   Ways to the church and manor court   59
   Lost lanes   59
   Stretes and Roman roads?   60

VI. Place-names, settlements and landscape   63
   Saxon origins   63
   A Bronze Age site?   64
   The Manor's Great Fields: Estfeld and Westefeld   66
   Estfeld land uses: sheep farming?   66
   Westefeld – and a lost hamlet?   67
   A nucleated village?   68
   Development 1600-1840 – a lost landscape   68
   Landscape clearance. A lost village?   69
   Changes within the Park   70
   Other lost places   70
   Lophams alias The Old House?   70
   A chantry chapel?   71
   Lost places outside the Park   71

Development 1840-1990   71
Appendix: Meanings and derivations   73

Glossary   94

References   99

Bibliography   102
    Documentary Sources   102
    Published Sources   102

Index of Personal Names   105

List of Subscribers   112

ILLUSTRATIONS

Maps in the text

1. Tithe Map of Woolverstone 1840 with field-names (pages 8-9). Redrawn for this book by Eleanor Leigh.
2. Map of the parish with field-names (pages 50-1). Drawn by Eleanor Leigh.
3. 'Map' of the manor 1350-1600 with place-names (pages 52-3). Drawn for this book by David Nuttall.

Plates

1. Extract from earliest surviving manor court roll, 1348. Reproduced courtesy of the Suffolk Record Office, Ipswich.
2. Extract from the court roll 1459. Reproduced courtesy of the Suffolk Record Office, Ipswich.
3. Extract from the first court of Thomas Wolfreston, 1495. Reproduced courtesy of the Suffolk Record Office, Ipswich.
4. Extract from court roll 1497: Oldtylhousyerd charter. Reproduced courtesy of the Suffolk Record Office, Ipswich.
5. Hodskinson's map 1783 (Shotley Peninsula) showing extent of Woolverston Park. Reproduced courtesy of the Suffolk Record Office, Ipswich.
6. (a) Map showing extent of Woolverstone Hall Estate 1937 (published with sale particulars, based on O.S. map) and (b) simplified location plan from *The Times* (2 December, 1937), published courtesy of Colin Hawes.
7. Plan of lanes from Woolverstone to Pin Mill 1807. Reproduced courtesy of the Suffolk Record Office, Ipswich.
8. Plan of Woolverstone Rectory and Glebe 1817. Reproduced courtesy of the Suffolk Record Office, Ipswich.
9. Aerial photograph of crop marks: West Field, Sandpit Field and Whinney Field, Woolverstone. Reproduced courtesy of the Royal Commission for the Historical Monuments of England.
10. Aerial photograph of crop marks in Cotton's Front Meadows, Newlands and Page's Common Fields – a large field in Chelmondiston. Reproduced courtesy of the Royal Commission for the Historical Monuments of England.
11. Aerial photograph of Woolverstone taken in 1994 and reproduced courtesy of the *East Anglian Daily Times*.

12 & 13. Aerial photographs of crop marks in Newlands and Page's Common Fields Chelmondiston. Reproduced courtesy of Suffolk County Council.

14. Aerial photograph of crop marks in Corner Field, Woolverstone. Reproduced courtesy of Suffolk County Council.

15. Aerial photograph of Park Field, Wolverstone. Reproduced courtesy of Cambridge University Collection of Air Photographs: copyright reserved.

16. Aerial photograph of Lower Park Field, Woolverstone, showing postulated Bronze Age burial mounds, tree-covered. Reproduced courtesy of the Royal Commission on the Historical Monuments of England.

17. Aerial survey photograph of the Woolverstone area in 1971. Reproduced courtesy of Aerofilms, Ltd. (copyright).

18. Tylhousyerd, Woolverstone: a kiln exposed on the Orwell river bank, summer 1991. Reproduced courtesy of John Newman.

19. Old Manor House, Woolverstone, pencil sketch, c.1776. Reproduced courtesy of the Suffolk Record Office, Ipswich.

20. Church of St Michael the Archangel, Woolverstone, before major alterations (engraving by H. Davy, 1838). Reproduced courtesy of the Suffolk Record Office, Ipswich.

21. Sisters of St Peter's Community outside the chapel at St Peter's Home, Woolverstone. Reproduced courtesy of St Peter's Community, Woking, and Jack Whitehead.

22. Interior of the chapel in St Peter's Home, Woolverstone. Reproduced courtesy of St Peter's Community, Woking, and Jack Whitehead.

23. Woolverstone Hall and the Cat House, early nineteenth-century engraving. Reproduced courtesy of the Suffolk Record Office, Ipswich.

24. The Widows' Homes, Woolverstone, 1994. Reproduced courtesy of Alan King.

Frontispiece

Woolverstone Hall. Drawing made by Gillian Read for the Babergh District Council *Woolverstone Hall Planning Brief*, reprinted by kind permission of the artist (page xii, facing page 1)

ACKNOWLEDGEMENTS

This work would not have been completed without the enthusiastic help and encouragement of Miss Gwenyth Dyke, former chairman of the Suffolk Local History Council. I also owe lasting gratitude to the lecturers who taught me, over the years, to understand and use documents both ancient and modern, to cope with the intricacies of palaeography, and to appreciate the peculiarities of medieval Latin – namely Mr Derek Charman, Mrs Marion Allen, Mrs Jo-Ann Buck and Dr John Ridgard.

The staff of the Suffolk Record Office have been most helpful in locating countless documents. I am grateful also to members of the Suffolk Archaeological Unit: John Newman, who encouraged me to explore the local fields and helped me to interpret what I found, and Edward Martin for his guidance on place-name derivations. Also, to all the local farmers who spared time to give me information about their fields, as well as to the many local residents who contributed memories of the Berners family and their estates in addition to facts about their own houses.

I am especially grateful to Norman Scarfe, who, after reading the 'final' draft, suggested improvements (and detected some errors) which I have been very happy to accept and correct. I appreciate his support more than I can express.

Dr Margaret Gelling, in her book *Signposts to the Past*, defines the study of place-names as a philological discipline distinct from those of history and archaeology. As an interested amateur, attempting to understand current place-name thinking and to apply it to illuminate the history of one small place in Suffolk, I am greatly indebted both to her and to the English Place-Name Society, whose publications have given me so much pleasure as well as enlightenment.

It is impossible to understand the evolution of a minor manor without reference to the history of the county in which it lay. *An Historical Atlas of Suffolk*, edited by David Dymond and Edward Martin and published jointly by the Suffolk County Council Planning Department and the Suffolk Institute of History and Archaeology, provides not only an indispensable source of facts but also a wide range of background information.

I thank Hilary Thomas for putting names on maps, David Nuttall for drawing the manor map, Eleanor Leigh for drawing the other maps, for shaping an untidy first draft and editing and rekeying the many revisions that followed, and Richard Leigh for generous technical support.

Thanks are also due, on behalf of the publisher, to John Field for his careful checking of the place-name derivations, and to Philip Riley for his usual meticulous proof-reading.

FOREWORD

It is a great pleasure to recommend Mrs Laverton's fascinating and detailed work on the place-names of Woolverstone. Good historical writing has always depended on the happy marriage of local facts with national history: we are all the product of the places where we have lived, moved and had our being, which we have shaped as they shaped us; human actions and names are engraved on landscape and memory with the same sharp edge. In turn each generation has been moulded by the movement of people, changes in farming, trade, wars, and travel far more than by formal education.

It has always been so; the place-names of a village reflect these changes. The most praiseworthy feature of this study is that many fleeting names have been identified and fixed, and the daily life of Woolverstone is enriched by these layers of human experience and endeavour so disclosed.

I hope that others living on the unique Shotley Peninsula will be inspired to record place-name lists for their own area. Not all will have the richness of documentation here – non-estate settlements may have fewer names on record, but retain the bonus of using their oldest still in this century. Names and the landscape could be changed beyond recognition in the next fifty years. Let us note them before it is too late.

Much credit is due to Mrs Laverton for producing this excellent book. In placing my personal congratulations before you, I trust that there will be many sequels from the land between the rivers.

G W Dyke
June 1991

INTRODUCTION

In 1977, in the course of a talk on field-names to the Suffolk Local History Council, John Field suggested that individuals and groups might undertake the collection, study and publication of Suffolk names. Undaunted by the magnitude of the task, a group of researchers began with the parishes of the Upper Deben Valley. These surveys have now been published by the Council in a format that allows comparison between the names on the Tithe Maps of *c.* 1840 and their present-day equivalents.

This book began as a corresponding survey for the parish of Woolverstone on the Shotley Peninsula. The existence of manorial and estate records provided the opportunity to enlarge its scope to include an outline history of the manor of Woolverstone Hall and its transformation by the Berners family into a picturesque Victorian model village.

The Tithe Map, showing field-names, and a sketch derived from the current OS map are used to illustrate the parish as it was in 1840 and as it is today. Notes explain changes. Probable locations for fourteenth- and fifteenth-century places have been deduced from documentary evidence and mapped. Together, these three maps show how Woolverstone has evolved over the past 550 years.

Place-names remain the central theme. The many names gleaned from documentary sources are listed alphabetically. In an appendix, derivations and possible meanings are proposed for most of these early place-names, many of which went out of use long ago. Some throw light on pre-Domesday Woolverstone, pointing back to Anglo-Saxon settlement in the seventh and eighth centuries. A more reliable interpretation of this obscure period awaits archaeological evidence from field-walking, metal detecting, aerial photography, perhaps even excavation. Already, by combining the small amounts of available information at present provided by these techniques, it has proved possible to explore landscape development in the Woolverstone area over long periods of time.

The study of place-names is a subject for specialists, but where names can be associated with a known landscape they add much to the interest of country walks and views seen from the river, besides providing material for armchair contemplation on winter evenings.

Knowledgeable readers will no doubt discover errors, omissions and shaky arguments: help in putting these right will be welcome.

Sylvia Laverton

Frontispiece: Woolverstone Hall. Drawing by Gillian Read

CHAPTER I

From Wolverston *Manor to present-day Woolverstone: 1300-1990*

The name Woolverstone in use today is the latest in a series that appears to have developed from *Wulfheres tun* meaning 'Wulfhere's farm'.[1] Exactly who he was and how and when he came to settle here remain obscure. There is a local legend telling of a Dane called Wulf who, en route to attack Ipswich, landed here and sacrificed a native on a large glacial stone 'for luck': hence 'Wulf's Stone' corrupted to Woolverstone. Nobody has ever found the legendary stone. The place is called *Hulferestuna* and *Ulverestuna* in the Domesday Survey (1086) and is named in an 1196 deed[2] as *Wolferston*. Norman Scarfe suggests to the author that if the name related to a large glacial erratic then, in the Domesday Book, it would have appeared as *Ulverestan*. Suffolk place-names now ending in -ston or -stone usually started as *-tuns*, although caution is needed in interpreting them, as he points out in his essay[3] on Suffolk place-names and settlements.

The 1327 Subsidy Return[4] groups Wolferston with neighbouring Chelmyngton. Variations in spelling – *Wulferston, Wolfreston, Wolferston* and *Wolverston* – occur in documents from the fourteenth century until the present spelling 'Woolverstone' was generally accepted from early this century. Except when quoting from early documents or referring specifically to the manor of Wolverston Hall, this modern spelling will be used in the survey.

Origins of manor and estate

The manor of Wolverston had its origins in Saxon times. When the Domesday Survey was made in 1086 there were two manors which later merged. This manor was larger than the parish. A document[5] surviving from 1419 records the findings of an inquisition in Ipswich to determine what lands had been held by Elizabeth de Wolferston when she died. The jury found that besides much else, she held for life 'a certain old manor called Wolverstonhalle with belongings in Wolverston and Chelmyngton and in the towns of Freston, Holbrook, Herkestede, Erwarton and Kyrketon'. That the jurisdiction of this manor did indeed extend to all the places listed is confirmed by the court rolls that record Woolverstone's manorial business.

The courts[6] held in 1349 and 1351 during the plague years show the medieval system more or less intact. After the Peasants' Rising in 1381 the surviving court rolls reflected a gradual decline in the power of the lords.

1

People grew more independent and unruly, failing to work on the lord's land as custom required, allowing their livestock to trespass on it, neglecting to attend the courts, illicitly cutting wood and buying and selling land without the court's permission.

The association of the Wolverston family with the parish and the manor lasted for at least three hundred years. Thomas de Wolverston headed the tax assessment list[4] when King Edward III was raising money in 1327 to finance his wars. Thomas's son Roger[7] held office as the King's Escheator in the three eastern counties of Suffolk, Norfolk and Essex between 1356 and 1369. He was also one of the Commissioners appointed in 1386 to supervise the Muster[8] in Suffolk. The next heir, also Roger, married Elizabeth Fitzraffe, who brought with her the lordship of *Wolverstonhalle* manor and this, with all her other lands, was inherited by Roger's brother Thomas. From that time the family held the manor until the last of their line, Philip, sold all to Sir Thomas Gawdy in 1555.

Thereafter, the manorial courts continued, but with diminishing authority, presided over by half a dozen families – Gawdy, Catelyn, Bacon, Parker, Bedingfield and Rous – none of whom stayed for more than two generations. Eventually the manor was bought by John Tyssen and mortgaged; he was already heavily in debt after losing money when the South Sea Bubble burst. His problems were not solved by assigning the mortgage to John Ward: by 1726 both were bankrupt.

Knox Ward claimed the manor in 1728, but when William Berners wished to acquire it, ownership was disputed and became the subject of a lengthy action in the Chancery Court. When, after nearly fifty years, the question was settled in 1773,[9] William Berners gained possession, but meanwhile the courts had lapsed[10] and the manor was virtually at an end. William Berners' son Charles tried to revive the courts but had to admit defeat. There appeared to be some legal justification for continuing but in practice it proved simpler for the Berners family to acquire land and property by outright purchase and to manage it without a regulatory court. In this way Woolverstone became the heart of the Berners estate which eventually extended over more than 6,000 acres in seven parishes throughout the Shotley Peninsula (Plates 6a, 6b). Thus the estate far exceeded in size the territory of the original manor. By the time the last of the family, John Anstruther Berners, lived in the Hall, lordship was long forgotten and he was known affectionately as Squire (Jack) Berners. He died in 1934. His son and heir Geoffrey Hugh Berners preferred to live in Berkshire and when the Woolverstone estate was sold in 1937 he moved to Little Coxwell Grove, Faringdon. He died in 1972, the last of the male line.

The Berners' architectural legacy

The Berners family were enthusiastic builders. Having purchased the estate, William Berners lost no time in providing himself with a fine new Hall to replace the old manor house, where he had been a tenant for some years. Bricks from this old house were used to build a stable block on the old site. The new mansion[11] overlooking the river Orwell was completed in 1776. John Johnson, who drew up the plans, was a London surveyor of Berners Street, Marylebone, where he had been developing land for the Berners family.

After William Berners died in 1783 his son Charles had an obelisk[12] erected in the Park as a memorial. This splendid landmark – it was ninety-six feet high and topped with a globe surrounded by rays – was accidentally destroyed by fire during World War II.

Although no relevant documents have survived, the pretty Gothic cottage called The Cat House near the river was presumably built for Charles Berners. Describing it as a folly, Barbara Jones[13] dates it as 1793, which is within Charles Berners' time. It is thought to occupy the site of a chantry chapel[14] and has a legendary association with smugglers and a cat. This remarkably biddable animal was, reputedly, placed in the window facing the river as a signal that there were no revenue men about, so that contraband could be landed safely. The story doesn't explain what happened when the cat – cat-like – chanced to stroll away. After it died, a more reliable system was adopted: the smugglers had the carcase stuffed and continued with that.

When these illicit deeds took place is never made clear, but they could not have happened in the Berners' time. Apart from the fact that this was a law-abiding family, the north, river-facing window of the 1793 Cat House was originally a large false one. It has a pattern of intersected tracery and painted on it is a grey and white cat; it seems that whoever designed it was well aware of the site's earlier history. Recent modifications have marred the simple elegance of this intriguing listed building, but the legend lingers on: a small white china cat sits on duty beside a newly glazed pane.

There are no mysteries connected with the other buildings in Woolverstone. Most were commissioned by John Berners after he inherited the estate in 1852. Development stemmed in part from the need to house the increasing number of people employed by the estate. It also reflected the desire of a wealthy Victorian family to enhance their surroundings while providing new and improved amenities for their tenants. First, a large house called The Homestead was provided for the land agent. Then came a project designed entirely for the estate owners' benefit: a new drive was made, extending from the Hall across Woolverstone Park to the river and on through Freston Park to emerge, via an avenue of copper beech trees, at the bottom of Freston Hill. The wrought iron gates there carry the initials

'JB' (John Berners), as also does the plaque dated 1861 on the south face of the gate house. This is Monkey Lodge, so named because a pair of stone monkeys stood guard on the gate pillars until Geoffrey Berners took them to his Berkshire estate. A stone shield on the lodge's north face displays the motto 'Del fuego el avola', commemorating escape from a fire at the Hall from which all were saved thanks to the warning clamour of the family's pet monkeys.

The new drive needed a second gate house where it passed through gates separating the deer in Woolverstone Park from Freston Park; it is still called Deer Park Lodge. The third gate house, Holbrook Lodge, guarded the main entrance drive to the Hall. It stands beside the main road through the village, opposite Glebe Lane, which provides the quickest way to Holbrook village. Perhaps more importantly at the time, this lane was also the way to Holbrook Gardens, a favourite place for sumptuous picnics by the lake.

As more and more people came to work in Woolverstone, the existing cottages became uncomfortably crowded. The need for more accommodation provided the opportunity to transform Woolverstone into a model estate village. This was accomplished without displacing tenants; any families who may have been removed from the Park area when it was enclosed some one hundred years earlier were by then no doubt well established outside the pale. From 1869, pairs of cottages, known as 'double-dwellers', were built beside the main Ipswich-Shotley road and, at the same time, most of the existing cottages were altered to look like the new ones. There was a new house (The Red House) for the schoolmaster, whose little village school was enlarged. A Clergy Rest Home was built to provide somewhat Spartan accommodation for over-worked parsons.

In the Park, a model dairy farm said to be copied from one on the Royal Estate at Sandringham was built in 1870 near the church. The circular dairy, fitted with marble-topped tables for cooling the milk and cream, was linked by a covered way with a pair of pretty half-timbered cottages. A small farmhouse nearby housed the cows.

After John Berners died, his brother Captain Hugh Berners RN added the Widows' Homes – a block of six cottages having the Berners coat of arms displayed on the front wall with the date 1877 and his initials 'HB'; stone monkeys decorate the corners of the roof.

The following year, drastic alterations to the church were begun. Henry Davy's engraving[16] published in 1838 depicts a short linear church with a single aisle, a squat west tower and a south porch (Plate 20). The original nave and chancel had been lengthened to designs by Sir Giles Gilbert Scott in 1862 but more space was needed, so Captain Berners commissioned the architects St Aubyn and Wadling to design what was in effect a new church.[17] It was completed in 1889 and dedicated to St

Michael and All Angels. Until then for hundreds of years St Michael the Archangel had been the patron saint.

The alterations involved pulling down almost all the original structure. Only the medieval tower (given new battlements and pinnacles), the fifteenth-century porch and the south wall were left. Nothing of the ancient structure was salvaged, so we shall never know whether the old roof tiles had been produced in the medieval tileyard by the river. Fortunately the porch, for which Robert Wolverston left 'halfe the brykkes and all the tymbyr' in his will in 1492,[18] was not demolished. It still stands.

While work went on at the church, The Berners Hall, its name inscribed in bold letters over the porch, was built to serve as a temporary church. This was the last addition to the model estate village.

Two more houses erected at the turn of the century completed the Berners' building activities in Woolverstone. One was the rather plain parsonage on Main Road (now Spring Lodge), the other the far from plain house-cum-chapel (Plates 21 and 22) designed by Edwin Lutyens.[19] The latter was built for use as a house of rest for the Sisters of St Peter's Community, an order then based in Kilburn dedicated to nursing and mission work in the East End of London. Charles Hugh Berners, who commissioned the house, was an Associate and trustee of the Order. St Peter's House, as it was then called, was occupied by the Sisters until it became a convalescent home for wounded soldiers during the Second World War; its subsequent history is outlined in the next chapter. By an odd quirk of history, this building, now under its more recent name of Woolverstone House, became linked with a London community: the North Westminster Community School Charitable Trust used it as a residential study centre for a short time. In the course of research into the history of the house, Jack Whitehouse has recently discovered that the building differs markedly in design from Lutyens' original drawings; he describes his findings in a pamphlet produced for the school.

After 1901 building in Woolverstone ceased for some sixty years. Although a few houses have been fitted in here and there since the estate was broken up in 1958 they are sufficiently unobtrusive to allow the village and its immediate surroundings to be designated a conservation area.[20]

The post-Berners years

In 1937 the estate was sold as a complete entity to the Nuffield Trust for the University of Oxford; the furniture in the Hall was auctioned and the building left to stand empty. Bidwells, the University's agents, took over the management of the estate. In 1939 the Royal Harwich Yacht Club negotiated a 99-year lease of the Cat House site but was unable to move there from Harwich until after the war.

5

Army units occupied the Hall and Park in 1942. In October that year the Admiralty took over, naming their 'stone frigate' HMS Woolverstone. As D-Day approached, HMS Woolverstone took part in a very secret disinformation operation code-named Quicksilver.[21] It was intended to deceive German intelligence about the location of the expected landing site for the invasion of France. Fake landing craft called Bigbobs were constructed in the park under cover of the trees and towed into the river to simulate part of the invasion fleet. To mislead German reconnaissance a full-scale Army encampment was simulated alongside the river, complete with sham wireless traffic with 21st Army Group HQ. This operation, backed by similar schemes elsewhere on the east and south coasts, pinned down a large number of German troops in the Pas de Calais area awaiting an invasion that in fact took place, as planned, on the Normandy coast.

After the war the Royal Harwich Yacht Club moved to the Cat House site, taking over two ex-Army Nissen huts and the concrete hard where a pier was built originally for the Berners' yachts – the yawl *Edith* and later the 83-ton schooner *Egret*. The present comfortable RYHC clubhouse designed by the Ipswich architects Peter Barefoot replaced the hutted accommodation in the late 1960s.

Austin Farrar had already established the adjacent Woolverstone shipyard, utilising the pier and hard constructed for the Royal Navy. There, many light-weight sailing craft were constructed by his cold-moulding technique. The first and most famous was the International 14 Windsprite K 583. After winning her first race – for the Prince of Wales Cup in 1950 – she went on to win it again three more times. Between 1973 and 1978 Woolverstone Marina was constructed to provide deep-water pontoon moorings, additional swinging moorings and all the necessary associated services. Long ago, this area beside the tidal Orwell estuary was home to a tiny community of Saxon farmers; today it is known to sailors from around the world.

The Hall became first a nautical training school,[22] then in 1951 the London County Council[23] announced plans to turn the Hall and park into an experimental state boarding school for boys. This venture proved successful academically until it was required to become a comprehensive school. The change brought a variety of problems, not least steeply rising costs said to exceed those of Eton College. The school closed in July 1990, after which the Hall and its extensive grounds were offered for sale subject to guidelines[24] prepared by the local planning authority. These are designed to prevent drastic changes, for the Hall is a grade I Listed Building. In June 1991 the Girls' Public Day School Trust announced that it had purchased the mansion and eighty acres of parkland for Ipswich High School for Girls, thus ensuring that the Hall's post-war connection with learning will be continued. The girls moved from Westerfield Road in Ipswich to their new site in the autumn of 1992.

Former parkland lying outside the Hall's grounds has now been absorbed into three farms, all of which spill over into neighbouring parishes just as in the days of the old manor.

Map 1: Tithe Map of Woolverstone of 1840, with field names

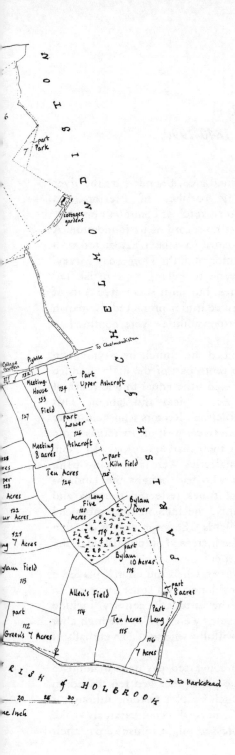

CHELMONDISTON

6

7 ⌐part
   Park

cottages,
gardens

To Chelmondiston

Cottage
Gardens   Pightle

132   Meeting-
      House   134 ⌐Part
      133   Upper Ashcroft
127   Field

122   ⌐Part Lower
      Meeting 126 Ashcroft
      8 acres
135
cres
per   Ten Acres
139   124
Acres
                    ⌐part
121   115 Kiln Field
ur Acres
             Long   Bylam
g 7 Acres   Five   110   Cover
             Acres
                          ⌐part
ylam Field   119   Bylam
113   10 Acres
                    118
             Allen's Field
                          ⌐part
part   114   117 8 acres
112   Part
Green's 7 Acres   Ten Acres Long
                   115   116
                          7 Acres

PARISH of HOLBROOK   → to Harkstead

20   25   30
e Inch

9

CHAPTER II
Woolverstone Parish: 1840-1990

Woolverstone parish today is a clearly defined area, bounded by the river
Orwell to the north, the neighbouring parishes of Freston and
Chelmondiston to west and east, with a short stretch of common boundary
with Holbrook parish in the south. There is no record of its foundation. A
parish – the area served by a parish priest – must have been associated with
Woolverstone's Saxon church, which is mentioned in the Domesday survey.

A tenth-century edict requiring everyone to belong to a parish led
generally to more clearly defined boundaries, but until successive Acts of
Parliament in the sixteenth and seventeenth centuries promoted the parish
as an area of secular administration, its responsibilities were confined to
church matters.

For a thousand years, lay people financed the church by payment in
kind. There was a praedial tithe equal to a tenth part of the main produce
of the land (corn, wood, hay, etc.) and a mixed tithe equal to one-tenth of
the produce of both stock (e.g. milk, wood, pigs) and labour. This
complicated system was open to several criticisms. Rectors who held more
than one living simultaneously were comparatively well-off, whereas some
curates had to find other work to augment their inadequate pay. In some
instances, tithes originally payable to monasteries were still being paid,
long after the dissolution, to the laymen who had bought the land. In
addition to these drawbacks, the value of tithes reflected the ups and
downs of farm production and so, inevitably, the income they produced
varied from year to year. Enterprising landlords who improved production
were still liable to hand over one-tenth of the increased output although the
church made no contribution to the capital spent.

Payment of tithes was never popular. Even when the church played a
central role in the spiritual life of every parishioner, avoidance occurred. In
Woolverstone as elsewhere, wills from the fifteenth century include
bequests that look like conscience money: sums were left 'to the high altar
for tithes forgotten', even in some cases 'wilfully withheld'. Eventually it
became clear that a new system was needed.

The Tithe Commutation Act of 1836 converted payment in kind to
payment in money, so that the rector of the parish received rent based on
the prevailing price of corn. This was a much simpler system, although it
too proved very unpopular in later years. Farmers who could scarcely make
a living when agriculture was severely depressed might refuse to pay their

10

meagre tithes, but if they did so they had to face the bailiff, who came with orders to seize property. Some villages still remember the resulting battles. In 1936 tithe rent charges were abolished; the Church Commission is now responsible for paying the clergy.

The Tithe Commutation Act required every parish to produce a large-scale map showing each piece of land liable to the new charge, together with a list of owners and occupiers. The latter was published as a schedule that defined the rent charge due for each field, garden and yard. Woolverstone parish was surveyed by John Spurling of Shotley. The parish copy of his map, dated 1840, is kept in St Michael's church in the care of the churchwardens. The Suffolk Record Office holds a second copy.[25]

Spurling found that the parish comprised 1028 acres subject to tithes, of which 490 were arable, 510 were meadow or pasture and 28 woodland. There was no common land. Nine acres of road were not chargeable. There were 30 acres of glebe. In that year the gross rent came to £239, payable to the rector of the parish, who at that time was the Revd Ralph Berners. The Revd Henry Denny Berners, in residence at the Hall, owned all but 50 or so acres of the parish land.

The Woolverstone Tithe Map and its present-day equivalent are disappointing sources of field-names. Many of those on the Tithe Map look suspiciously like names assigned by lawyers and surveyors involved in the transfer of land to the estate. No doubt Baker, Barker, Scarfe, Marston, Mason and the others had names for the fields they sold, but they are listed simply by the former owners' names and the acreages.

Few names have survived from 1840: Dench Wood, Glebe Wood, Glebe Field and Corner Field can still be found. Pratt's Shrubbery remains; likewise Handkerchief Field (now much enlarged) and Ashcroft Field under its present name of Ashcraft. West Field, in 1714, lay on both sides of the common way footpath; by 1840 the northern part had been divided into Sandpit Field and Whinney Field and these names are still in use. The southern part was known as Hog's Trough in 1840, but is now called West Field again. Where several fields have been amalgamated since 1840, the new ones sometimes have names which refer to transient features such as Barn, Pear Tree, Pony and Kennels. Football Field is now arable, the game being played elsewhere. Stackyard and Meadow Fields survive in name, although neither stackyard nor meadow now exist on these sites. Big Field was surely named when inspiration failed. White's and Fisk's refer to the recent occupiers of houses built on those fields.

The Tithe Map and present place-names
In the table of names which follows, the numbering is the same as that in the original schedule, which was arranged to group occupiers together, except when present fields have been made by amalgamating several of the old fields.

1840 Tithe Map no. & name	Present and earlier names
1 Churchyard	Churchyard and church of St Michael and All Angels (formerly Archangel).
2 Hall, out offices, yards	Woolverstone Hall boarding school (to 1990) with two additional blocks for kitchens, classrooms and dormitories built in the 1970s.
3 Stables, sheds, yards	The nineteenth-century stables, which stood on the site of the old manor house, were converted to flats during the 1960s. A water tower rises above the central gateway; tennis courts and a disused swimming pool are nearby; also the small former slaughter-house and game store. Otter hounds were kennelled in the old stable block in Squire Jack's time.
4 Part of Park	Cricket pitch and pavilion.
4a Lodge and garden	The old lodge was replaced in the mid-1860s by a new lodge (Holbrook Lodge) and drive.
5 Part of Park, south of Iron Fence	Six fields: Pear Tree, Barn, Pony, Football, Twelve Acres, and Vic Hill's. Football is now played elsewhere. Vic Hill lived in a cottage across Main Road.
6 Part of Park, east of Iron Fence	Part of Hall grounds.
7 Part of Park owned by Lucas	Part of Park Field; Lucas also owned land in neighbouring Chelmondiston.
8 Cottage and garden; tenant Abraham Pollard	A pair of cottages known as Park Cottages.
9 Plantation	Plantation
10 Saltings	Saltings, now much eroded.
11 Cat House	Cat House, now enlarged and altered.
12 Cliffs and Plantation	The Cliffs are badly eroded along the shore; some trees were felled in the 1960s, and there is no trace of the nineteenth-century carriage drive through rhododendrons.
13 Paddock and workshops	The Dairy House, gardens and paddock; converted in the late 1980s from the pair known as Dairy Cottages, which were built in 1870. During the 1950s the southern cottage served briefly as the village police station.
14 House, Yard and Garden; tenants Thomas Matthews and another	A small dairy farm dating from 1870 remains in use on part of the site formerly occupied by an eighteenth-century rectory. Charles Berners exchanged this land, together with TM13 and former glebe land, for land outside the Park.
15 Nursery	Farmyard
16 Plantation	Sold in the 1960s as a building site; now occupied by The Garden House, Bourne View, Ridgeway, Half Acre and The Studio.

17	*with* 17a, 17b, 17c	These now form part of Paul Double's Nursery Gardens. In the 1970s a house was built next to Main Road called Walhfof (meaning 'with a little help from our friends').
18	Pightle	Now also incorporated into Paul Double's Nursery Gardens.
22	Buildings and yards	Formerly an estate cottage by the roadside, and the estate yard occupied by carpenters, black-smiths *et al*. Pre-Berners there was a shop and warehouses. The estate cottage has been renamed Sideways Cottage and the site is now occupied by Millwood, The Chippings, Timbers, The Old Barn and The Old Forge.
23	Great Lodge Field	In the north-west corner, a house with a chapel, designed by Edwin Lutyens, was built in 1901 for St Peter's Community; used by convalescing soldiers in WW II; then leased as a private house called in turn The Oak House, Woolverstone House, White's and, as a dormitory for Woolver-stone Hall School, Corners (after the first house-master). As Woolverstone House again, briefly a study centre for the North Westminster Comm-unity School Charitable Trust. On the Main Road side stand: The Red House and The Hollies (formerly The Clergy Rest Home, then Hamilton House). In adjacent former Parkland are post-war houses: Parkside, Little Park, The Old Police House, Springfield and Crosswinds. The field between the footpath and Main Road is now called White's.
24	Pratt's Shrubbery	Deer Park Lodge and gardens have occupied the northern area beside the river since the 1860s. The plantation dating from the 1920s at the southern end was considerably damaged by a severe gale in October 1987; the central part was felled in the 1970s and replaced by poplars. Pratt himself was probably an estate forester.
29	Alder Carr	Alder carr
30	Last's Meadow	Still known locally as Last's Meadow, although it is now parkland; it has a spring and several specimen trees including a Wellingtonia (*Sequoiadendron gigantea* BUCHOLZ). Last was an estate tenant in the nineteenth century.
31	Rough	This is now part of Freston Park; its surface is uneven. Terracotta shards litter the river edge, evidence of the tile yards which operated here in the fifteenth century. The boundary with the adjacent parish of Freston lies along the bed of a

		stream which was known in the sixteenth century as *Prestylbrook*.
32	Part Great Alder Carr	Alder carr
33	West Field	Now Sandpit and Whinney Fields without a dividing hedge; they are bounded to the north by Whinney Field Wood, mainly conifers planted in 1943.
34	Hog's Trough	Now called West Field, it lies adjacent to Mannings Lane with Stackyard Field behind Home Farm. In the seventeenth century it was possibly known as *Hobbs Croft*. Five pairs of Victorian estate cottages, Nos 5 to 14, lie alongside the main road. Nos 7 and 8 now form a single dwelling.
38	Part Barn Meadow	This is now part of the paddock behind Home Farm; there is no barn now.
39	Stack Yard	Stackyard
40	Pightle *and* House, buildings and garden (41)	Both are now incorporated into Pig's Pightle.
42	Buildings, yard, etc.	Home Farm, buildings and yard
46	Part Ten Acres	Part Garden Field
47	Eight Acres *with* Part Payne's Field (47a) *and* 49, 49a *and* Nine Acres (50)	These six fields together now make up Orchard Field. Part of 50 is also included in Handkerchief Field.
53	Denches Wood Field	Dench Wood Field, also known as Dents.
56	Denches Wood	Dench Wood; earlier *Densshwoode, Densewoode, Dennysshwode*.
79	Upper Ball Field *with* Part Upper Ball Field (79a) *and* Klopfer's Cover (80)	Part of Lodge Field behind the site of the Ball Inn. There are no trees here now.
81	Twelve Acres	Also now part of Lodge Field.
82	Eleven Acres	Fisk's; named for Kenneth Fisk whose house Threeways was built in 1938 on the corner of Main Road and Harkstead Lane. In the 1960s The Wick and The Holt were built alongside Main Road adjacent to Threeways.
82a	Part Eleven Acres	Also now part of Fisk's.
85	Little Lodge Field *and* Ball Field (86)	Both are incorporated into Lodge Field.
89	Cook's Pond	Still extant; it was cleaned out in the 1980s.
97	Old Corner Field	Corner Field
119	Bylam Cover	Bylam Wood
101	Barn, garden and drift	Since disappeared.
135	Spaces between Road and Park Paling *with* Long Five Acres (120) *and* Ten Acres (124) *and* Part Kiln Field (125)	These four fields have been amalgamated to form Seventeen Acres. Kiln Field was in Chelmondiston and was bought by Berners from John Leggatt in 1838.

126	Part Lower Ashcroft *and* Meeting Eight Acres (127)	These two were combined to form Ashcraft.
130	Driftway	Disappeared
133	Meeting House Field	Now part of Ashcraft. Its name refers to the cottage used for meetings of Woolverstone Baptists before they moved to Stoke Green, Ipswich in 1773; it was bought by Berners in 1805, but then disappeared.
134	Part Upper Ashcroft	This has also been taken into Ashcraft.
50	Nine Acres *with* Handkerchief Field (51) *and* Five Acres (52) *and* Little Denshes (57) *and* Leggatt's Pightle (58) *and* Cottage (59) *and* Garden (60) *and* Mason's Six Acres (61) *and* Part Little Denshes (62) *and* Part Parker's Eight Acres (63) *and* Part Parker's Hill (64) *and* Barker's Six Acres (65) *and* Part Scarfe's Meadow Drift (66) *and* Part Scarfe's Eight Acres (67)	All combined to form Handkerchief Field; ironically, the name probably implied a very small field. Part of 50 was included in Orchard Field.
69	Mason's Fourteen Acres *with* Green's Seven Acres (70) *and* Stonepit Field (71)	All form First Hall Field
74	Barker's Ten Acres *with* Ten Acres (75)	Now make up Second Hall Field; there is no hedge between this and First Hall Field.
76	Part Thirteen Acres *with* Thirteen Acres (77)	Now called Eighteen Acres, to include five acres of former glebe land.
100	Dickerson's Nine Acres	Kennels Wood
102	Driftway	Since disappeared.
103	Upper Glebe Wood Field	Glebe Field
104	Holton's Glebe *with* Glebe Wood (105)	Glebe Wood
106	Lower Glebe Wood Field *with* New Pasture (107)	Both now form part of Big Field.
108	Wood Meadow *with* Barn Meadow (109)	Both now make up Stackyard Meadow.
110	House, buildings, yard, garden	White House Farm, yards, etc.

111	Marston's Eight Acres *with* Part Green's Seven Acres (112) *and* Bylam Field (113) *and* Allen's Field (114)	Four fields now amalgamated to make up Stackyard Field.
128	Five Acres	Kennels Field
129	Chimpton Close	Now Kennels Field. Chimpton, also Chempton, is an abbreviation of Chelmondiston.
122	Four Acres	Part of Big Field
123	Upper Five Acres	Part of Big Field
25	Cottage and garden; tenant David Cook	Replaced by a double estate cottage, since converted to a single dwelling, No. 2 Mannings Lane.
19	A garden	Garden of Spring Lodge
20	House, buildings, yard and garden	Spring Lodge: from the 1980s an old people's rest home; formerly the parsonage, built 1901.
21	House and yard; tenant Robert Mills and another	Incorporated into Spring Lodge.
26	Garden; tenant John Podd	Now belongs to No. 2 Mannings Lane.
26a	Cottage; owner Jeremiah Webster	Now a pair of cottages, Nos 3 and 4 Mannings Lane. The original owner stoutly resisted Berners' offers to buy until he secured an agreement in 1842 to retain the cottage for his lifetime.
27	Cottage and garden; tenant Charles Johnson	
28	Cottage and garden; tenants George Hill and another	Now Nos 1 and 2 Deerpark Cottages, at the foot of Mannings Lane.
83	A garden; tenants Charles Addison and another	A Victorian Estate cottage.
37	Cottage and garden; tenant Robert Gibbs	Victorian Estate cottages were built on this site; now Nos 9 and 10 Main Road.
43	Cottage and garden; tenants John Elmer and another	Former double-dweller Estate cottage, now Nos 3 and 4 Main Road.
44	Cottage and garden; tenants John Scarfe and another	Former double-dweller Estate cottage, now Nos 1 and 2 Main Road.
59	Cottage and garden; tenant Samuel Reeve and another	No building extant, simply part of Handkerchief Field.
60	A garden	Part of Handkerchief Field
68	A garden; tenant Benjamin Catchpool	Three cottages now stand on the site.

84 Cottage and garden; tenant Samuel Stuart — The Berners Hall. Built in 1888, it was given to the parish as the village hall by Geoffrey Berners in 1965. Formerly called The Reading Room.

90 Cottage and garden; tenant Susan Lucas *with* Cottage and garden; tenant William Eaton (91) *and* Cottage and garden; tenant William Winney (92) *and* Cottage and garden; tenant Robert Goose (93) — Victorian Estate cottages now occupy this site as Nos 24 to 27 Main Road. Number 24 housed the Woolverstone telephone exchange in Mrs Pryke's kitchen from 1910 until 1954, operating round the clock during the war years 1939-45. Number 27 is called Wisteria Cottage.

98 A garden *with* Cottage and garden; tenant William Head and others (99) — Now Nos 30, 31 and 32 Main Road occupy part of the site; they were originally the estate laundry. Next, standing back from the road, is The Old Kennels, the Agent's house pre-1937. Adjacent is The Gables, built in the 1960s on the site of the game-keeper's kennels.

94 Cottage and garden; tenant William Warren — Nos 28 and 29 Main Road and the former village school occupy this site.

94a Cottage and garden; tenant Mary Boreham

131 Cottage and garden; tenant Mary Grimwood and others — A pair of listed timber-framed cottages not reconstructed during the Berners days, now Nos 33 and 34 Main Road; 34 is undergoing modernisation (1991).

132 Pightle; tenant and Thomas Webb — Two pairs of Victorian cottages, Nos 35 and 36, 37 and 38 Main Road; Cecil Crack was born in No. 38 and still lives there (1991).

87 Ball Inn Garden and Yards — The inn was once part-owned by John Cobbold the Ipswich brewer. On the site now stand the Widows' Homes.

35 Pightle; tenant John Bird — Still a garden, Mannings Lane.

36 Cottage and garden; tenants Charles Addison and another — Rebuilt as an Estate cottage; now Nos 13 and 14 Main Road.

88 Gardens; tenants John Leggett and others — A row of three Victorian Estate cottages now occupies this site as Nos 21, 22 and 23 Main Road; a house was built in the 1970s between No. 23 and Cook's Pond (TM 89).

78 Little Ball Field — Part of Lodge Field

89a Part of Upper Ball Field — Part of Lodge Field

72 Cottage and garden; tenants David Allen and others — Cottages, Nos 3 and 4 Harkstead Lane

73 Cottage and garden; tenant Robert Driver and others — Cottages, Nos 1 and 2 Harkstead Lane

17

6a	Part of Meadow	
115	Ten Acres *with* Part Long Seven Acres (116) *and* Part Eight Acres (117) *and* Part Bylam Ten Acres (118)	Combined to form Bylam Field. The remainder of 118 went into Stackyard Field.
45	Part Sage's Pightle	Now in Garden Field.
54	Part of Swampey	Hedges were realigned to take this into Dench Wood Field.
55	Part of Great Denches	Also now part of Dench Wood Field.
96	Schoolhouse Field	Glebe land later exchanged.
77	Part of Thirteen Acres	Taken into Eighteen Acres.
95	Gardens	Still allotment gardens.

CHAPTER III
Wolverston *to Woolverstone: place-names 1300-1840*

Place-names retrieved from manorial and other records show how complex the land changes in Woolverstone have been since 1300. A very large number of the earlier names went out of use a long time ago, although many known in the fifteenth and sixteenth centuries can be placed, approximately, on a map.

In the fourteenth century, farming methods had already begun to move away from the classic highly organised manorial system. This was based on arable fields (the Great Fields, with names such as Westfeld and Estfeld), with common grazings in wood-pasture, fens and marshes. Meadows supplied hay, and heath and woodland provided both fuel and building materials. Crofts and closes gradually invaded the earlier more open landscape and the place-names of the period reflect these changes. From the turn of the sixteenth century, men whose ancestors had held land 'for service', or more freely but still 'at the lord's will', were acquiring their own farms and calling themselves yeomen.

Manor courts continued until 1727 but their value as a source of place-names declined. From about 1600, changes in holdings were recorded by naming the tenants rather than places. The development of the Berners' Woolverstone estate produced new sources. Many deeds, mortgages, affidavits, abstracts of title and miscellaneous correspondence include place-names relating to land transactions from the seventeenth to the nineteenth centuries.

Glebe Terriers provide names from 1636 until 1813. Probate records (from 1444 to 1700) also mention place-names. All these sources are available in the Suffolk Record Office in Ipswich. Other useful sources are to be found in the Public Record Office and the Diocesan Records held in the Norfolk Record Office.

Names gleaned from all these sources are presented here with notes on their origins. In discovering and collecting place-names the local historian experiences all the excitement, frustration and occasional enlightenment inherent in any form of detective work. Exploring their meanings requires a different approach, for names reflect the changing relationships between places, the people who lived there and the language and dialects they spoke. Interpreting place-names therefore demands linguistic skill as well as imagination and a good knowledge of the local terrain. This aspect of the names listed here is dealt with fully in the appendix, which is arranged alphabetically for ease of cross-reference with the list below. A few terms that occur frequently are explained in the glossary.

The following abbreviations have been used:
CR   =   the court roll;
f   =   the order of the folios (membranes) in the court rolls: the 45 membranes that make up the earlier roll are fastened together in a way that obscures the details required for exact dating, so the regnal years quoted are not absolutely accurate;
Ct Bk   =   the Court Book;
GT   =   the Glebe Terrier.

Alder Carr	A field of alder carr, one acre, sold by Christopher Newham to Samuel Lucas as part of Runtings in 1714. *S1/10/4.9*
Affosswalle	Two pieces of land in Affosswalle were included in land conveyed by charter from Henry Gawdy to Thomas Bramston in Chelmondiston. *CR.f.37 32 Eliz. 1590*
Alcots	John Chapman (alias John Felton of Kirkton-Shotley) was fined, owing suit of court for the holding. *CR. f.17 10 Hen. VII 1495*
Ames	A tenement with four acres. *S1/10/11.5 1631*. Documents both earlier and later refer to the same place as Emmes.
Arnold's Fen	Formed the western boundary of 12 acres to which Thomas Snell was admitted. *CR. f.15 6 Hen. VII 1491*
Ashcraft	The same as Ashcroft below; it is now part of White House Farm.
Ashcroft	Upper (five acres) and Lower (eight acres) Ashcroft lie on the eastern edge of the Woolverstone/Chelmondiston boundary and were part of Rudlands Farm, bought by Berners. *S1/10/1.1 1845*
Badylond	John Neweman paid a rent of 2*d*. for pasturing two horses here. *CR. f. 22 Ed. III 1348*
Bakelers Grove	Thomas Cook ordered to do fealty. *CR. f.14 3 Hen. VII 1488*
Bakelerslands	Lay south, west and east of nine acres (three pieces) of land, bounded to the north by the King's Highway from Ipswich to ffishbane. *CR.f.16 7 Hen. VIII 1492*

20

Bakers Field Six acres sold in 1628 by Philip Catelyn to William Andrewes, an Ipswich mariner. Eventually it passed to William Berners and formed part of the original Berners estate. It lay east of 'the driftway to the shore'. *S1/10/3.4*

Baldwins Nine acres of meadow and pasture with a messuage and tenement, conveyed by John Bugg to John ffen. *Holbrook Ct Bk 1702-1713 S1/10/9.11*

Bark Field Three acres sold by Christopher Newham to Samuel Lucas as part of Runtings in 1714. *S1/10/4.9*

Barn Field Two and a half acres sold by Thomas Stisted to Robert Munnings, together with a barn and cartlodge. It was formerly owned by Francis Danske. *S1/10/4.5 1718*

Barnecroft Occupied by Thomas Juferby of Herksted. *CR. f.28 14 Hen. VIII 1523*

Barnfield on the hill Five and a half acres sold by Christopher Newham to Samuel Lucas as part of Runtings in 1714. *S1/10/4.9*

Bataylles Grove A wood held of the manor by Margaret Bataylle, daughter of John Bataylle. *CR. f.21 17 Hen. VII 1502.* Two people were fined for felling six oaks in this wood. *CR. f.18 11 Hen. VII 1496*

Bernecroft The rector, John Rybely, conveyed this land by charter to John Pykesome for *4d.* rent and two days' service. *S1/10/11.3 1502.* It was described as John Culpho's and lay next to Bramappilion. *CR. f.22 20 Hen. VII 1505*

Bickmores A ninety-eight acre farm in Chelmondiston and Harkstead bought as 'the manor or capital messuage called Pusills or Pesills' by Charles Berners in 1789. Documents include an extent with field names. *See also* Peselys etc. *S1/10/10.7*

Birchcroft / Byrchecroft One and a half acres adjacent to land formerly held by Nicholas Runtyng granted to Rose Ingram. *CR. f.16 5 Hen. VII 1491.* With other lands it was granted to Elizabeth Wulferston, widow, and defined then as lying in Chelmondiston, between land of Nicholas Runtyng to the west and Sampson to the east. *CR. f.33 22 Hen. VII 1508*

Blithes A tenement held by John Briggs. *CR.f.14 3 Hen. VII 1488*

Boldwennes Pightle / Boldwynes The boundary of land sold to Thomas Bakeler under the terms of Edward Latymer's will. *S1/14/3.3 1544*

Boldyrods — John Candysshe admitted to a tenement and one piece of land called Boldyrods and le Vant. *CR. f.13 1 Hen. VII 1485*

Bordmales — A holding in Freston later called Petts or Tylers. *HE7:2855 deed 1567*

Bottoms *or* Wasteland — Ten acres, part of lands sold by Charles Boone to William Berners, described as having the meadows of Goulsdon and the Tower Shore to the west and Old House Cliffs to the east. *S1/10/3.1 1749*. These ten acres appear to be Dunton Fennes, sold with a messuage by Philip Catelyn to William Andrewes. *S1/10/3.1 1628*

Bradcroft — A close between the King's Highway to the south and Fletcherfeld to the north, granted to Thomas Conyers. *CR. f.22 20 Hen. VII 1505*

Bradstok — A croft in Chelmondiston granted to John Busshman's heirs. *CR. f.4 3 Hen. IV 1402*. A piece of land in Bradstok called Grenecroft, formerly Busshman's and granted to Roger ffuller. *CR. f.15 5 Hen. VII 1490*

Braham — Lands in Braham; subject of a quit claim by John Cukhook with Robert Caketon of Wolferston in 1410. *Hervey, Gr Bk xvi(2)*

Braky Heath / Breaky Heath / Breaky Hill — Land formerly associated with Water Shape and Willy's Land, part of a tenement in Freston occupied by William Barker, sold by Edmund Knappe to Barnaby Burleigh in 1707. *HE7:2855 abstract of title*. Defined one head of a holding called Truefords. *CB 1711*

Bramappilion — A thirty-acre croft for rent of 3s. at Easter and Michaelmas, between church land on the east, John Culpho's Piksomers on the west, one head on Churchewey and the other on John Culpho's Bernecroft. *CR. f.22 20 Hen. VII 1505*

Bramacroft — A manor holding. *CR. f.2 22 Ed. III 1348*

Brampstons — Thomas Brampston was admitted to one grove comprising one and a half acres of woodland, to the north of the King's Highway and with its western boundary on Mowslowe Lane, also known as Brampston's Lane. *CR. f.15 5 Hen. VII 1490*

Bramstons Lane *see* Mowslowe Lane

Bramstonslands — Roger Fuller admitted to three acres called Bramstonslands. *CR. f.29 16 Hen. VIII 1524*

Brattucks — A seven-acre field included in an 1830 schedule of estate lands. *S1/10/4.1*

Bridges — A tenement called Bridges left by Richard Snell to his son John. *Will January 1620/21 S.Rec.Soc xxxi 1990.* Edward Snell, miller of Chattisham, conveyed Bridges to Henry Fairbrother, yeoman, of Freston: one messuage, one cottage, one barn, one stable, six acres of land and two of pasture. The Ipswich-Shotley road lay to the south and Westfield to the north. *S1/10/11.20 (title dates from 1689)* See also Brygges

Broad Oaks — Probably the same land as Brattucks. An eight-acre field among manor lands sold in 1628 by Philip Catelyn to William Andrewes. Eventually William Berners acquired it from Charles Boone and it was taken into Woolverstone Park. *S1/10/3.4*

le Brodefeldys — Two pieces of land in Freston among lands conveyed by charter to Robert Sherman. *CR. f.7 1 Hen. V 1413*

Brodestok — Richard ffybet was fined for withholding rent for this croft in Caketon. *CR. f.22 20 Hen. VII 1505*

Broome Close — The southern boundary of woodland conveyed to Thomas Bakeler under the will of Edward Latymer. *S1/14/3.3 1544*

Broome Hill — A field of one and a half acres bought from James Sewell by William Berners. *HE7:2855 1765*

Bryckeffylde / Bryckphylld — Two acres in Sowthefeld sold with other land in Freston and Woolverstone under the terms of Edward Latymer's will. *S1/14/3.3 1544*

Brygges — Robert Hewarde was free tenant of this holding. *CR. f.30 18 Hen. VIII 1526*

Bylams — A farm in Chelmondiston occupying ninety acres in 1990; formerly part of Pesills; and *see also* Bickmores.

Bylands — Forty acres of land 'Bylams otherwise Bylands' sold in 1728 with a messuage called Pinmill. *T4/16/1*

Cages — Eight acres bounded by the Ipswich-Woolverstone road to the north and divided by the parish boundary with Freston. Charles Berners acquired the land in 1817 as a garden with 120 fruit trees and 400 gooseberry and currant bushes. *S1/10/11.9 (title from 1689).* In 1990 it was part of Garden Field.

Caketon — Subject of a quit claim in 1410 involving Robert Caketon of Kyrketon (a Domesday manor: Shotley) *re* lands in

Braham. *Gr. Bk xvi(2)*. A tenement and land held by Thomas Brandeston of Chelmondiston reverted on his death to the manor 'i.e. Caketon and Lopham'. *CR. f.2 22 Ed. III 1348*. Sheep and lambs recorded on pasture in Caketon. *CR. f.2 22 Ed. III 1348*. A croft in Caketon formerly occupied by Robert Busshman. *CR. f.4 3 Hen. IV 1402*. Elizabeth Wolverston held a tenement called Caketon in the town of Wolverston with belongings there and in Chelmyngton, Herkested and Holbrook. *IPM 1419 PRO 7 Hen. V 50; trs. Hervey Gr Bk xvi(2)*

Caketonheth   Two heaths comprising 40 acres granted to William Smyth at a rent of 13*s*. 4*d*. *CR. f.12 38 Hen. VI 1460*

Caketon Croft   Twenty-eight acres, described as lying in Holbrook, ffreston and Harkested, were held by Thomas Ingram at the time of his death. *CR. ff.27, 28 14 Hen. VIII 1523*

Caketon Yerd   John Smyth held Caketon Croft next to Caketon Yerd. *CR. f.31 19 Hen. VIII 1528*

Calves Pightle   A one-acre field included in a schedule of manor land. *S1/10/4.1 1830*

Calveton Street   Land held of Woolverstone manor in Calveton Street (Shotley) was granted to Sir Calthorp Parker's heir. *CR.f.40 1612*

Chappell Land   Richard Snell bought this land from William Cawell (Hayle?) and bequeathed it to his son Richard. *Will 1583 SRO CC/AA1/24/252*

Chekers   Seven pieces of manor land 'in Chekers' were included in the charter below.

Chelendelondys / Chelendlondes   Land in Chelmondiston granted to Richard Brome. *CR. f.26 12 Hen. VIII 1521*. Forty-one acres lying in Langlond conveyed by charter from Henry Gawdy to Thomas Bramston. This land was next to Bramston's land abutting westwards on Estfeld otherwise Falegatefeld. Other named pieces of land included in this charter were manor lands in Chelmondiston. *CR. f.37 32 Eliz. 1590*

Chelmondiston-Santon   Richard Wolverston's holdings included those in Chelmondiston 'held of the Bailiff and Chamberlain of Chelmondiston Santon'; that is, a water mill, 40 acres of land, 20 acres of pasture and 10 acres of woodland. *Inqu. PRO. C 142/61/33 1537*

Cherdowne — Part of a parcel of land conveyed by charter from Henry Gawdy to Thomas Bramston: '3 pieces in Cherdowne and 3 roods *in valle* in said Cherdowne', with much else. *CR. f.37 32 Eliz. 1590*

Church Field — Seven and a half acres included in a schedule of estate lands in *S1/10/4.1 1830*, but just five acres in three pieces on the north side of the church in *GT 1636*.

Churchewey — Boundary of a thirty-acre holding called Bramappilion. *CR. f.22 20 Hen. VII 1505*

Chyrchecroft — One acre, bounded by Emmesway to the west and the footpath to Ipswich on the south, let with other land to Thomas Snell for rent, a brace of mallard and two brace of teal. *CR. f.15 6 Hen. VII 1491*

Clappers — Twelve acres. Richard Fibet was amerced; he owed suit of court. *CR. f.22 20 Hen. VII 1505*

le Cley — Richard Mabesyn was fined for digging and removing a cart- load from the lord's land, le Cley. *CR. f.3 1 Hen. IV 1399*

The Cliff — Ten acres next to Great Hill abutting on Dunton's Meadow to the west. It was sold by Philip Catelyn to William Andrewes, who sold to Richard Bowele; eventually it came into the hands of the Berners and was taken into Woolverstone Park. *S1/10/3.1 1628-1749; S1/10/3.4 1636*

Colecroft — Land called Colecroft in Shottele formerly enfeoffed to Roger atte Perye. *CR. f.2 22 Ed. III 1348*. Colecroft lay below land called Synthons, possibly a different croft. *CR. f.14 4 Hen. VII 1489*

Commonfeld — Sheep grazed in Commonfeld. *CR. f.2 22 Ed. III 1348*. Robert ffuller was fined for taking 30 loads of fodder from Commonfeld. *CR. f.11 37 Hen. VI 1459*

Copts / Captens Corner — Crossway on the Woolverstone-Shotley road. *GT 1706*. Corner Field in 1980s?

Cortledownffen / Curtledownffen / Furtherdown Fen — The western boundary of Newcroft. *CR. f.44 1635; Ct Bk 1672, 1774*. The names were used indiscriminately in the relevant documents.

Crabbe Trees — An orchard in Pesehyl; John Burcham of Holbrook stole apples and was amerced. *CR. f.5 7 Hen. IV 1406*

Crane's Heath   The eastern boundary of land sold under the terms of Hugh Lord's will in 1624. *Suff. Rec. Soc. xxxi 1990*

Crossespyghtle   Land held for service by John att Hell; its sale without licence was recorded in the Court Roll. *CR. f.5 7 Hen. IV 1406*

Cukkowyd   One acre of woodland with a messuage sold by charter. *CR. f.12 38 Hen. VI 1460*

Curtelisdonlands   The boundary of land formerly belonging to Roger Wolfreston, in the neighbourhood of Dunton Walton. *CR. f.13 38 Hen. VI 1460*

Cussowood   A holding of Thomas Sampson in Freston/Woolverstone. *CR. f.35 24 Hen. VIII 1533*

Danecroft   Thomas Juferby amerced for breaking hedges above the lord's Danecroft (in Chelmondiston) and illicitly cutting alders for stakes and firewood. *CR. f.32 19 Hen. VIII 1528*

Demensures Heath   The western boundary of land sold under the terms of Hugh Lord's will in 1624. The land was in the neighbourhood of Crane's Heath. *Suff. Rec. Soc. xxxi 1990*

Dench Wood / Densshwode / Densshwood   A wood on the boundary between Woolverstone, Freston and Holbrook parishes, still known (1990) as Denchwood. Sheep and lambs were recorded grazing in Densshwode. *CR. f.2. 22 Ed. III 1348.* Trespass with sheep in the lord's pasture at Densshwood recorded in *CR. f.5 7 Hen. IV 1406*; similarly in *CR. f.21 17 Hen. VII 1502* and again in *CR. f.26 12 Hen. VIII 1521.* Denchwood occupied sixteen acres in 1609. *Will, Edmond Knapp, PRO 20 Wyngfield 1610.* In 1980 it contained oak, sweet chestnut as old coppice, elm mainly along part of the boundary, holly, several large geans (wild cherry), hawthorn, elder, crab trees, larch, bracken, brambles, bluebells and honeysuckle. There were no banks or ditches; its extent is now four acres.

Dennysshwode   Trespass in the alnet (alder grove) within this wood recorded. *CR. f.27 15 Hen. VIII 1524*

Doneton   Nicolas de Doneton assessed xiid in the Subsidy Return of 1327. *Gr Bk ix. See also* Donton *and* Dunton

Donnegrove   A small grove granted to John and Rose Hetham at Chelmondyst Chyrche Gate in Chelmondiston. *CR. f.14 3 Hen. VII 1488*

26

Donslon Street One boundary of a messuage and tenement called Joyners. *S1/10/3.4 1761; S1/10/11.18 1827*

Dontonstrete A way leading from Dontonstrete to Salt Water described as the eastern boundary of a twelve-acre pasture. *CR. f.15 6 Hen. VII 1491*

Donton Walton John Candysshe was admitted to pasture in Donton Walton (with other land: le Vant, Boldyrods and Jonescroft). *CR. f.13 38 Hen. VI 1460.* Thomas Culpho was amerced for neglecting ditches at Donton Walton. *CR. f.13 38 Hen. VI 1460*

le Downe Philip Hetham was recorded as owing suit of court for le Downe. *CR. f.15 5 Hen. VII 1490*

Downynnge William Bramston owed suit of court for this holding. *CR. f.19 12 Hen. VII 1497*

Duck Marshe Seven acre adjacent to Waterclose in Freston. *HE7:2855 deed 1567*

Dunton Fennes Part of the manor land held by Elizabeth de Wolverston. *IPM 1419 7 Hen. V 50.* A ten-acre fen with messuage, manor land sold by Philip Catelyn in 1628; bought by William Berners in 1749. *S1/10/3.1*

Dunton Meadows Part of the manor land held by Elizabeth de Wolverston. *IPM 1419 7 Hen. V 50.* Two meadows amounting to two acres, sold with Dunton Fennes.

Duntons Pightle Listed with Dunton Meadows. *S1/10/4 1749*

Dunton Wastes Lay 'above Westfield'. *CR. f.13 1 Hen. VII 1485*

Elbury Down The eastern boundary of two acres of land with a messuage, conveyed to William Bugge of Holbrook by Robert Glanfield. The west boundary was on the 'common way to the strand'. *S1/10/4.5(10) 1683*

Elderobordes One toft and two pieces of land for rent at 3*d.* per annum, held by Ada Pondere of old, then by William Alcott; on his death it reverted to the manor. *CR. f.4 3 Hen. IV 1402; CR. f.5 7 Hen. IV 1406*

Elves Acre The northern boundary of three closes called Emmes. *CR. f.36 1 Mary 1543.* A tenement which lay north of Emmes, held by Nicholas Snell. *CR. f.42 1624*

Emmes / Emms (*see also* Ames). Three closes known as Emmes, with Elvesacre to the north, rented to Thomas Candysshe for 8*s.* 8*d.* per annum. *CR. f.22 20 Hen. VII 1505.* Nicholas

Mason held this land; his three daughters later inherited one-third each. *CR. f.42 1624.* The land was sold with other manor land by Philip Catelyn to Philip Bacon in 1628. After many changes it was eventually united in Berners ownership. *S1/10/4.10*

Emmscroft   Ten acres in Freston (Lambards or Spetmans) sold under the terms of Edward Latymer's will; it lay between Emmscroft or Emms and land of Freston manor. *S1/10/3.3 1544 (See also* Lambards)

Emmysway   The western boundary of Chyrchecroft. *CR. f.15 5 Hen. VII 1490*

Emryngales   Land and tenement sold by John Fuller. *CR. f.14 3 Hen. VII 1488.* Richard Wolverston held land in Chelmondiston of the bailiff and chamberlain of Chelmondiston Santon, 1537.

Estfeld   A common field called Estfeld appears in a charter conveying lands held of Woolverstone manor in Chelmondiston from Henry Gawdy to Thomas Bramston. *CR. f.37 32 Eliz. 1590*

Falegatefeld   A field in Chelmondiston mentioned in Henry Gawdy's charter. Also known as Estfeld. *CR. f.37 32 Eliz. 1590*

ffyshbane / Fishbane   There are many references to the road from Ipswich to Fishbane, synonymous with the King's Highway. For example, William Wade was amerced for allowing stock to stray on to it. *CR. f.13 38 Hen. VI 1461.* Evidence has been adduced by Hervey for a hamlet in the Shotley area. *Hervey, Gr Bk xvi (2) 1912*

ffive acres   Two acres of land and one acre of pasture called Ffyveacres. *CR. f.16 7 Hen. VII 1492*

Fleshers / Fletchers / le Fletchers Field   Lucy Bramston, widow of Roger, admitted to Fletchers. *CR. f.16 7 Hen. VII 1492.* Le ffletchersfeld is the northern boundary of Bradcroft. *CR. f.22 20 Hen. VII 1505.* Thomas Bramston sold ffletchers to Thomas Cukkok. *CR. f.33 22 Hen. VIII 1531.* A tenement in the field called Gt Shambles. *S1/10/11.1(1) 1619*

le ffoulewater   Thomas Candysshe and Thomas Annyng, clerk, amerced for taking clay without a licence from Watershepe and le ffoulewater. *CR. f.6 11 Hen. IV 1410*

Four Acres / Fower Acres   A four-acre field 'lately occupied by Francis Danske' sold by Thomas Stisted to Robert Munnings. *S1/10/4.5 1718*

Foxall / Foxalls / Foxhill Field   A five-acre field at one time owned by Francis Danske and sold by Thomas Stisted together with other lands to Robert Munnings. *S1/10/4.5 1718*. In 1628 it was among land sold by Philip Catelyn to William Andrewes, and in 1749 it was eventually acquired by Berners. *S1/10/3.1 1628-1749*

Foxall Lane / Foxhole Lane A way: the southern boundary of a close called le Poynt, part of Longstokheth. Now Glebe Lane. *CR. f.22 20 Hen. VII 1505*

Frith Heath   Abutting north on Fishbane Way with one head on Sir Thomas Felton's Truefords. *Ct Bk 1711*

le ffullyngmell   Situated in Chelmondiston and offering evidence of cloth making. Thomas Juferby diverted water from it by blocking 'a certain porta aquatica called watyryatte' and was amerced. *CR. f.27 14 Hen. VIII 1522*

ffullyngmyll Pasture   In Chelmondiston; occupied by Thomas Juferby (see above) and formerly by Robert Fuller. *CR. f.27 14 Hen. VIII 1523*

Further Alder Meadow Four acres sold by Christopher Newham to Samuel Lucas as part of Runtings in 1714. *S1/10/4.9*

Further Field   A three-acre field bought by Thomas Stisted with two other fields. *HE7:2855 1719*

Furtherdown ffen   *see* Cortledownffen

Gibbis Fen / Gibbs Fen Candysshe's land called Gibbisfen was the western boundary of a close called Pecks or Peckcroft. *CR. f.22 20 Hen. VII 1505*

Godfreys   *see* Pecks

Godfrey's Pitell Thomas Candysshe admitted. *CR. f.23 23 Hen. VII 1508*

Godmancroft   Mentioned only as the boundary of an unnamed grove in the neighbourhood of Mowslowe Lane, otherwise called Bramston's Lane. *CR. f.15 6 Hen. VII 1491*

Grace's Lane   *see* Tracey's Lane

Gravel Pit Field A two-acre field sold with other closes, making 26 acres in all, by Benjamin Glandfield and John Allen to Jonathon Rosier. *S1/10/11.27 1716*

Great Hill / *possibly also* / Sand Hill *and* Side Hill A five-acre field next to The Cliff, sold by Philip Catelyn in 1628 to William Andrewes, who sold it to Richard Bowel (Bowle) in 1636, when it was described as four acres 'sometime with broome'. *S1/10/3.4.* Sand Hill in a schedule of estate lands and Side Hill in *S1/10/3.1* 1749 appear to be the same field. *S1/10/4.1 1830*

Great Sandford Eight and a half acres sold by Christopher Newham to Samuel Lucas as part of Runtings in 1714. *S1/10/4.9*

Greneacre A tenement in Chelmondiston held of Woolverstone Hall manor. *CR. f. 44 1635*

Grenecroft A croft in Bradstock, formerly John Busshman's. *CR. f.15 5 Hen. VII 1490*

Gretedown Margaret Cook was admitted to this land, formerly held by John Hetham. *CR. f.16 7 Hen. VII 1492. See also* le Downe.

Grotesclose Three pieces of land otherwise called *Metherdonffeld*, conveyed by charter to Robert Sherman; formerly held by Lawrence and Agnes Pod. *CR. f.7 1 Hen. V 1413*

a Grove Three acres of woodland sold to Thomas Bakeler under the terms of Edward Latymer's will. *S1/14/3.3 1544*

Grystmel / Grystmelles Walter ffuller admitted to a piece *in campo* called *Grystmel. CR. f.2 22 Ed. III 1348.* John Bakeler left two mills called *Grystemelles* to his son William. *Will 1481 SRO IC/AA/2/3/1*

Hall Lane Formed the north and east boundaries of four pieces of glebe land (?Church Field) amounting to four and a half acres whose western boundary was 'land going down to the cliff'. *GT 1706*

Handkerchief Field Identified on the 1840 Tithe Map and still known (1990) by this name although the field itself is now considerably larger.

Hanging Hill Field One acre at the end of Well Meadow; sold by Philip Catelyn to William Andrewes in 1628. *S1/10/3.4 1628*

Hare and Hounds Comprised yards and two cottages, part of which was owned by Christopher Rolfe and the Smith family, and part by Parker, an Ipswich brewer. In complex transactions the Berners acquired part in 1827 and the remainder from John Chevallier Cobbold of Ipswich in 1862. It was not shown as a public house on the Tithe Map. *S1/10/11.18; S1/10/11.27*

Harecroft   A close and pightle in Peselh, amounting to six acres lying below Wardesclose, granted to John Warburton. *CR. f.11 37 Hen. VI 1459*

Harpells   *see* Sharpells

le Harrow   Together with Poy Field it made up four acres; the southern boundary was on Old Strete Lane from Wolverstone to Harkstead. It was sold to John Bakeler under the terms of Edward Latymer's will. *S1/14/3.3 1544*

Heathlands   Ten acres of heath in Woolverstone and Chelmondiston, let to Roger Smyth. *CR. f.3 1 Hen. IV 1399*. In the seventeenth century the manor lands included 200 acres of heath and furze (*S1/10/4.5 1628*); by 1830 only 10 acres were listed. (*S1/10/4.3 1830*); when the Berners estate was sold in 1937 there was none left.

Heath Grounds   Grouped with Kettlescroft. *S1/10/4.1-4.4 1705-1720*

Heggyngwode   Thomas Juferby was amerced for damage. *CR. f.31 19 Hen. VIII 1527*

le Herreyplett Two acres, formerly John Barker's. *CR. f.23 2 Hen. VIII 1511*

Higher Alder Meadow   Two acres sold by Christopher Newham to Samuel Lucas as part of Runtings in 1714. *S1/10/4.9*

The Hills   Associated with New Croft as 'New Croft or The Hills'. There are two round, tree-covered shallow mounds slightly higher than the surrounding ploughland near the site postulated for New Croft.

Hobbescroft   Let to Thomas Candysshe for rent. *CR. f.23 23 Hen. VII 1508*

Hobbs Croft / Hob's Croft / Hobbies Croft   A close belonging to Francis Danske; the north head was on Westfield and the south head on the common way from Fishbane to Ipswich. *Ct Bk 1658*. The area was defined as two acres. *Ct Bk 1777*

Hog's Trough   Shown on the Tithe Map lying between the common way and Main Road. From the 1980s it has been part of West Field.

Holbrook Lane Piece   A three-acre field sold to Robert Munnings by Thomas Stisted in 1718; listed with former Danske land in a schedule of estate lands. *S1/10/4.9 1830*

Holchoncroft   One of four pieces of land in Chelmondiston granted to the widow Elizabeth Wulferston. It was bounded on the

31

north by the King's Highway from ffishbane to Gippeswyc (Ipswich). *CR. f.33 21 Hen. VIII 1531*

Hopp Ground   One acre with a driftway sold by Christopher Newham to Samuel Lucas as part of Runtings in 1714. *S1/10/4.9*

Howners   Glebe land included one acre next to a house called Howners which abutted on its south side on the road to Ipswich. *GT 1636*

Howthencroft   A croft granted with other land to Rose and Richard Ingram; its south side was next to the King's Highway. *CR. f.15 6 Hen. VII 1491*

Hulverscroft   Part of a parcel of land including Kewes which amounted to 10 acres; Foxall Lane was on the east and Oldstreteway to the south. Timothy Dalton, rector of Woolverstone, bought it with other lands from Philip Catelyn in 1621 and later sold it to Christopher Hayward. *S1/10/11.2 series; S1/10/11.7 1655-1725*

Jirnetts   Robert Giles admitted to land called Jirnetts or Reds. *CR. f.16 8 Hen. VII 1493*

Jonescroft   John Candysshe admitted to this croft, which lay above Westfield, at a rent of 3d per annum. *CR. f.13 1 Hen. VII 1485*

Joyners   Richard Snell left a tenement 'lately purchased' to his son Richard. *Will 1583 SRO IC/AA1/27/252.* Acquired by Charles Berners, and described as a cottage 'now two dwellings' lying on the corner of Donslon Street and the Ipswich-Fishbane road. *S1/10/11.27 1826*

le Kelne   Occupied by Thomas Pitman; the eastern boundary of a pightle called *Oldtylhousyerd. CR. f.19 12 Hen. VII 1497.* See also Tylhousyerd *and* Tylkyll

Kettles Croft   Mentioned as 13 closes comprising 60 acres in an abstract of title in lands sold to John Tyssen. S1/10/11.13 1720; also in *S1/10/4.6 1686-1720*; included in a schedule of manor lands. *S1/10/4.1 1830*

Ketylscroft   The southern boundary of Wulfelondcroft. *CR. f.21 17 Hen. VII 1502*

Kewes Croft   The eastern boundary of two pieces, each of one and a half acres, the western boundary being Oldstreteway and the southern the way from Herksted to Ipswich. Kewescroft was in Longstokheth. *CR. f.15 6 Hen. VII 1491.* Sold by Dalton with Hulverscroft; the boundaries were then east

on Foxhall Lane, south on Oldstreteway. *S1/10/11.2 1636.*
Evidence of title is recorded in *S1/10/11.7 1655-1725.*

Kine Slade   A charter from Henry Gawdy to Thomas Bramston included a piece in Kine Slade in Chelmondiston. *CR. f.37 32 Eliz. 1590*

Kinnelfeld   One and a half acres in this field included in Henry Gawdy's charter conveying land in Chelmondiston to Thomas Bramston. *CR. f.37 32 Eliz. 1590*

Klondyke   Part of the Woolverstone Hall gardens.

Lambards or Spetmans   Ten acres in Freston north of the tenement known as Lambards or Spetmans were sold to Thomas Bakeler under the terms of Edward Latymer's will. *S1/14/3.3 1544.* A tenement called Lambards or Spetmans is mentioned in the marriage settlement of John Goldson and Sarah Reynolds. *S1/10/11.4 1684.* It was among several pieces of land in the marriage settlement of John Gouldson (*sic*) and Ann Muddyclift. *HE:2855 1711.* Listed with land which Berners bought from the Parker family. *S1/10/11.8 1827*

Lane Croft   John Bakeler left this together with Strepecroft to his son Richard. *Will 1481 SRO IC/AA/2/3/1*

Langlond   Forty-one acres called Chelendlondes are described in the charter of Henry Gawdy to Thomas Bramston as 'in Langlond' in Chelmondiston. *CR. f.37 32 Eliz. 1590*

Langstoc / Longstok   Sheep were pastured there. *CR. f.2 22 Ed. III 1348*

Last's Meadow   Named on the 1840 Tithe Map; later taken into Woolverstone Park.

le Lees   A close. *CR. f.26 12 Hen. VIII 1521*

Litil Down / Litledowne   William Bramston to do fealty for this land in Woolverstone and Chelmondiston formerly held by John Heth. *CR. f.16 7 Hen. VII 1492.* The charter from Henry Gawdy to Thomas Bramston included three pieces of land and another half-acre. *CR. f.37 32 Eliz. 1590*

Litill Lophams A two-acre croft held by George Clerk. *CR. f.25 4 Hen. VIII 1513*

Little Hilly Field   Three and a half acres sold by Christopher Newham to Samuel Lucas as part of Runtings in 1714. *S1/10/4.9*

Little Sandford Field   Two acres sold by Christopher Newham to Samuel Lucas as part of Runtings in 1714. *S1/10/4.9*

Lockum Field   Four and a half acres included in a schedule of manor lands. *S1/10/4.1 1830*

Longstokheth   With Kewescroft it made the eastern boundary of one and a half acres abutting on the Herkstead to Ipswich way on the south. *CR. f.15 6 Hen. VII 1491*. Included a close called le Poynt. *CR. f.22 20 Hen. VII 1505*

Lophams   Lophams in Freston and Woolverstone was held of Holbrook manor by Henry Gawdy for a rent of 20*s*. *Hol. Ct Bk. 31 Eliz. 1579*. In 1628 a messuage called Lophams with outbuildings, appurtenances and sixteen acres was sold by Philip Catelyn (then lord of Woolverstone manor) to William Andrewes, an Ipswich mariner. All acquired by William Berners in 1749. *S1/10/3.4*

Lopymfeld   The Rector of Wolferston was amerced for 'making an unjust way leading to the lord's land called Lopymfeld'. *CR. f.2 22 Ed. III 1348*

Mabbesdonfeld   A capital messuage, 12 acres of pasture and two fields lying in a certain field (*in campo*) called *Mabbesdonfeld*. *CR. f.3 1 Hen. IV 1399*

Malt House / Malting Office   A mortgage by John Driver, maltster, concerns one messuage and malthouse. *HE7:2855 1680*. It was later acquired by William Mellsupp and conveyed in 1720 to John Tyssen. In 1723 a mortgage by Mason and John Ward to Robert Bacon, carpenter, listed a house, mill and waste adjacent, abutting on Cliff to the west, Old House to the south-east and thence to two posts leading to a close towards Woolverstone Hall, and east and north to the lower watermark of the river Orwell, with Malt Offices on said waste ground 'intended to be built'. *S1/10/4.11*

Malting Offices   Included with buildings, barns and land with the capital messuage called Runtings, sold by Christopher Newham to Samuel Lucas in 1714 (at Pin Mill, *q.v.*). *S1/10/4.9*

Marchams / Marchamts   Land and a tenement in Chelmondiston let at a rent of 3*d*. per annum. *CR. f.14 3 Hen. VII 1488*

le Marsshe   James Mynt amerced for trespass with pigs in *le Marsshe* and at *le Lees. CR. f.27 14 Hen. VIII 1523*

Mary's Croft   Thomas Felton Bt. was the freehold tenant of this croft bounded on the east by 'Mary's Lane'. *Ct Bk 1711*

Mary's Lane   The southern boundary of Lockum Field which lay east of Church Field and Old House Road; land sold by Philip Catelyn. *S1/10/3.1*

Meeting House A Berners Estate Book (no longer available) records the purchase of the Baptists' Meeting House by Charles Berners from Rouse, Cooper *et al.* in 1805.

Meeting House Field   Named on the 1840 Tithe Map. The site of the meeting place of a group of Baptists formed in Woolverstone in 1757. Joseph Sage and Stephen Bruce, who was related to the Pain(e) family (see entry below), were deacons; services were held at the Cat House. The group moved to Ipswich in 1773, forming Stoke Green Baptist Church.

Meeting House Yard   This amounted to a half-acre yard, three pieces of land, a barn 'lately blown away' and the land on which the Meeting House stood. It was sold by Elizabeth Paine to Charles Berners and then to Henry Denny Berners following Charles' death in the course of negotiations. *S1/10/11.19-24 1716-1839*

Melwantway / Melwantwey A way in Freston; John Sargent was amerced for not repairing the hedges and fences. *CR. f.31 19 Hen. VIII 1528*

Mere Field   Sold to Henry Pett and described as lying between Chappell Field and Dench Fields (in Freston) with one head on the east abutting on an ancient way to Dench Wood, part of lands including Mere Field, Dench Marshes and Water Close. *HE7:2855 Deed 1567*

Mershmans   A thirteen-acre tenement, land and pasture. *CR. f.13 38 Hen. VI 1460*

Metherdonffeld *see* Grotesclose

Moresheth   Thomas Heyward amerced for trespass with cows and calves. *CR. f.12 38 Hen. VI 1460*

Mormans Pightle   Included in a charter conveying land formerly held by Lawrence and Agnes Pod to Robert Sherman. *CR. f.7 1 Hen. V 1413*

Mowslowe Lane   Also known as Bramston's Lane, the eastern boundary of a grove belonging to Thomas Bramston. *CR. f.15 5 Hen. VII 1490*

Musemelne   A mill situated in Chelmondiston, demised by Hugh de Braham to Gilbert de Raimes. *HD/1538/181 Ph.N.35902 and with no other details*

Myddefen / Myddelffen Grazing land for cattle and horses. *CR. f.2 22 Ed. III 1348; CR. f.6 11 Hen. IV 1410*

Newbrygge   Four acres included with lands sold under the terms of Edward Latymer's will. *S1/14/3.3 1544*

Newcroft *or* The Hills   Nine acres rented to Thomas Candysshe. *CR. f.22 20 Hen. VII 1505.* Nine acres sold to Thomas Bakeler under the terms of Edward Latymer's will. *S1/14/3.3 1544.* Elizabeth Barker held New Croft at the time of her death. *CR. f.44 1627.* It was surrendered to Robert Danske; its western boundary was defined as Cortledowne fenn (*Ct Bk 1658*); it was passed to Francis Danske. *Ct Bk 1672.* In a schedule of estate lands its boundary was given as Furtherdown Fen. *S1/10/4.1 1830*

Newecroft   A manor holding. *CR. f.2 22 Ed. III 1348*

Newestrete   One rood of land at Newestrete abutting on the King's Highway granted to Alice, daughter of Thomas Bataylle. *CR. f.8 4 Hen. V 1417*

Newhalle   A tenement with garden and curtilage and a small grove called Donnegrove at Chelmondyst Chyrche Gate, granted to John Hetham and his wife. *CR. f.14 3 Hen. VII 1488*

Newholke / la Newholke de Hanburgh / ?Hammburgh   The tenant (not named) was amerced 40*s.* for taking in 20 perches of land below his house at Wolferston. *CR. f.14 4 Hen. VII 1489*

Northsterche   Two acres in this field were part of a large number of fields in Chelmondiston which Henry Gawdy granted by charter to Thomas Bramston. *CR. f.37 32 Eliz. 1590*

Old House   Mentioned in the delineation of Malt House land. *S1/10/4.11 1723*

Old House Cliff   This lay east of 10 acres called Bottoms or Wasteland. *S1/10/3.1 1749*

Old House Field   The eastern boundary of Sand Hill (Side) Field. *S1/10/3.1 1749*

Old House Lane The southern and eastern boundaries of Church Field, which was among land bought by William Berners from Charles Boone. (Sand Hill *alias* Side Fields was another boundary.) *S1/10/3.1 1749*

Oldstrete Lane   The northern boundary of land sold under the terms of Edward Latymer's will; the lane led from Woolverstone to Harkstead. *S1/14/3.3 1544*

Oldstreteway   The western boundary of one and a half acres having Longstokheth on the east and the Herksted to Gyppeswic road to the south. *CR. f.15 6 Hen. V 1491*

Over the Way   One of thirteen closes called *Kettles Croft*. *S1/10/11.13 1720*. It was listed as three acres in a schedule of estate lands. *S1/10/4.1 1830*

Pailor Field / Tailor Field   Three acres in the schedule of estate lands. *S1/10/4.1-4.3 1830*. As 'Tailor' it was included in land conveyed from Thomas Stisted to Robert Munnings; it was previously owned by Francis Danske. *S1/10/4.5 1718*

Pakermarsshe / Pakersmarsshe   A marsh; James Mynt amerced for poaching hares. *CR. f.27 15 Hen. VIII 1523*

Parkway   Berners' name for the road from the Cat House to Main Road. Recently it has also been known as the Cat House Road; it leads to Woolverstone marina and the Royal Harwich Yacht Club.

Pascarwode   William Frost amerced. A fine was imposed for depositing rubbish at Pascarwode. *CR. f.31 20 Hen. VIII 1529*

le Pasker   Many tenants amerced for trespass with grazing animals and pigs. *CR. f.9 2 Hen. VI 1423*. John Candysshe amerced for laying nets to trap duck ('wild mallardys') and other wild fowl at le Pasker and taking birds valued at 20*s*. *CR. f.11 37 Hen. VI 1459*. Le Pasker is described as the boundary of three acres 'below rectory close', the other head being on the King's Highway. *CR. f.11 37 Hen. VI 1459*

Pear Tree Close   Three acres mortgaged by Henry Bowle to Thomas Thurston were described as having Pear Tree Close on the north and west. *S1/10/1.14 1743*

Pear Tree Field   Exists at the present day; abuts on to the footpath from Woolverstone Church to Chelmondiston and has Woolverstone Park's Nelson Avenue on the west.

Peckecroft   Four messuages and a croft called *Peckecroft* were conveyed by charter to John Fuller. *CR. f.7 1 Hen. V 1413*. A six-acre close let to John Candysshe next to his Gibbisfenn. *CR. f.22 20 Hen. VII 1505*

Pecks or Godfreys The western boundary of six acres situated between Cages and the King's Highway and abutting on Dench Wood. *S1/14/3.3 1544*

Peschelles Phillip Sukkook (?Cukhook) amerced for unlicensed wood-cutting in the lord's coppice. *CR. f.9 2 Hen. VI 1423*

Pesell Six and a half acres of land comprising a close and pightle in Pesell. *CR. f.11 37 Hen. VI 1459*

le Pesells One 'grovetta' and one adjacent field amounting to twelve acres adjacent to le Pesells. *CR. f.23 23 Hen. VII 1508*

Peselys Grazing land for sheep. *CR. f.2 22 Ed. III 1348*

Pesfyllyd Seven large pigs recorded as grazing here. *CR. f.12 38 Hen. VI 1460*

Pesills / Pusills Described as an 'unidentified manor in Chelmondiston' (*S1/10/10.6*) but located as a ninety-eight acre farm in Chelmondiston, Harkstead and Woolverstone purchased by Charles Bramston from the Hamblin family in 1789. When Berners bought it he called it Bickmore's, after the occupier. *S1/10/10.6 and 10.7 1789.* Bylams Farm now occupies the site.

Pesselclose / Peselclose Fifteen acres in three pieces granted to John Smythe, abutting on the common way from Herksted to Ipswich on the west. *CR. f.13 1 Hen. VII 1485.* Fifteen acres granted to Margaret Smyth, widow of John. *CR. f.31 19 Hen. VIII 1528*

Pesyllys Grazing land for sheep. *CR. f.12 38 Hen. VI 1460*

Petts and Tylers The subject of a mortgage in trust for Samuel Lucas; there were no identifying details. *S1/10/11.27 1734.* Much more detail in a long abstract of title. *HE7:2855 documents 1567-1849*

Peytenmynes The tenant was amerced, owing suit of court. *CR. f.2 22 Ed. III 1348*

Pickostane Lands which were the western boundary of a messuage conveyed by John Wyles of Harksted to John Crane of Wolverstone. *S1/10/11.6 1643*

Picks / Pinks Four acres mentioned in John Goldstone's marriage settlement (*S1/10/11.4 1684*) and also in John Gouldson's. *HE7:2855 1711*

Picksomes / Piksomers   The western boundary of 30 acres called Bramappilion of which the eastern boundary was manor land with one head on Chyrcheway and the other on Bernecroft. *CR. f.22 20 Hen. VII 1505*. Mentioned in James Pylburgh's will in 1542/3 as a house and tenement 'with all its free and copy lands'. *Gr Bk xvi(2), p. 86*

Pin Mill   Land in Pin Mill (this may be an error as it appears to relate to land in west Woolverstone). *CR. f.42 1624*. A messuage called Pin Mill mortgaged by Miss Mary Lucas of Stratford in Gloucestershire, daughter of John Lucas; part of a legacy from her father. *HD.352/1-2 1781*. John Wells of Ipswich was amerced for breaking into the lord's house at Pyn Myll and stealing 12 beer barrels ('xij berbarells'). *CR. f.20 13 Hen. VII 1498*. See also le ffullingmell

Podds *or* Poytwynd   Thomas Snell was admitted to two pieces of land for an annual rent of 2*s.* 4*d.* Previously held by Elizabeth, former wife of Simon Hervey. *CR. f.15 5 Hen. VII 1490*

Pompards   Seven acres let to John and Margaret Smyth. *CR. f.13 1 Hen. VII 1485*

Potts Pightle   This was among land conveyed from Thomas Stisted to Robert Munnings, in a block formerly occupied by Francis Danske; it went later to William Berners. *S1/10/4.10 1718*

Poy Field   *see* le Harrow

le Poynt   A close, part of Longstok Heth, with its southern boundary on Foxhole Lane. *CR. f.22 20 Hen. VII 1505*

Prestylbrook   A stream, marking the western boundary of a pightle called *Oldtylhousyerd*. It forms the parish boundary between Freston and Woolverstone. *CR. f.19 12 Hen. VII 1497*

Prinnys   A messuage held by Nicholas Snell. *CR. f.23 23 Hen. VII 1508*

le Purlieu   The western boundary of land called Mary's Croft. *Ct Bk 1711*

Purtepyt / Purtepet   A lost manor in Samford Hundred, recorded in the Suffolk Domesday Book: 'Sixty acres held before 1066 by Osbern freeman of Ælfric the priest; there were always three villagers, two smallholders, two slaves, half a plough in the lordship and two men's ploughs.' It came under the jurisdiction of East Bergholt and the tax due amounted to ten shillings. 'In 1086 the same Osbern holds.' Walter Purtepet grazed cows in the lord's pasture. *CR. f.2 22 Ed. III 1348.* William Purtepet grazed lambs and sheep. *CR. f.5 7 Hen. IV 1406.* Thomas Purpet of Ipswich was amerced 40*s.* for poaching pheasants in land of Woolverstone manor. *CR. f.17 10 Hen. VII 1495.* William Tendryng Esq was amerced, owing suit of court for Purpette and Purpetyd. *CR. ff.17&19, 10&12 Hen. VII 1495-97 and other courts to 1500*

Pusills / Pesills   A ninety-two acre farm sold by Robert Sparrowe of Ipswich to John Mann, mariner, of Ipswich and described as 'all the manor and site of the manor or capital messuage' in a deed including field-names. *S1/10/10.7 1663*

Quinns   Three pieces formerly owned by Francis Danske, in a schedule of estate lands. *S1/10/4.1 1830*

Rainbow   Part of two acres formerly owned by Francis Danske sold by Thomas Stisted to Robert Munnings. *S1/10/4.5 1718.* One acre listed in a schedule of estate lands. *S1/10/4.1 1830*

Rectory Close   Mentioned in relation to le Pasker but with no clear indication of its location. *CR. f.11 37 Hen. VI 1459*

Reds   *see* Jirnetts

Robyns Close   The southern boundary of a field called Poy Field or the Harrow. *S1/14/3.3 1544*

Rocketts Grove   William Peckman was amerced for trespass in coppice wood. *CR. f.6 11 Hen. IV 1410.* A grovetta (little grove) called Rocketts in Freston/Woolverstone was let to Thomas Candysshe. *CR. f.23 23 Hen. VII 1508.* Three acres in two pieces mentioned in the Gouldson marriage settlement. *HE:2855 1711*

Runtyngs / Runtings   William Bramston distrained to do fealty for 'land and tenement formerly Runtyngs, held of this manor'. *CR. f.14 3 Hen. VII 1488.* A 'capital messuage' with sixty acres, conveyed by Christopher Newham to Samuel Lucas with malting offices and other buildings; later all was acquired by the Berners estate. *S1/10/4.9 1714.* This property appears to be the messuage called 'Pin Mill, with forty acres called Bylams and malting premises', mortgaged by Miss Mary Lucas. *HD 352/1-2 1781; T4/16/1 1782*

Sand Hill Field / Side Hill   Appears in a list of fields bought by William Berners; four acres abutting west on the driftway to the shore, north on Bottoms, east on Church Field and south on Lockums. *S1/10/3.1 1749*. Included in a schedule of estate lands. *S1/10/4.1 1830*

Sandpettes   A fine for trespass in the lord's land at Sandpettes is recorded. *CR. f.2 22 Ed. III 1348*

Sarjents / Sarjeants Heath   Six pieces or closes, pasture and heath, sold by Philip Catelyn in 1621 to Timothy Dalton, rector of Wolverstone, for the sum of £40. *S1/10/11*. Abuttals in *S1/10/11.4* suggest that the land lay beside Foxall Lane (now Glebe Lane). John Sargent was amerced for trespass in pasture and for neglecting fences on Melwantwey. *CR. f.31 9 Hen. VII 1528*

Sebbyngcroft   Three acres of pasture in Harksted or Chelmeton: the description is unclear in the original document. *CR. f.3 1 Hen. IV 1399*

Gt Shambles   Bond of Robert Meadowes, shipwright, of Ipswich, relating to a piece of pasture belonging to a tenement called Fletchers in the field called Gt Shambles. *S1/10/11.1(1) 1619*. Two and a half acres of land called Gt Shambles 'with messuage lately built' were sold in 1636 by Timothy Dalton to Christopher Hayward, jun. The boundaries were: east, a rectory field called Shambles; west, Foxhall Lane; south, Lt. Shambles; and north, the Ipswich to Fishbane highway. The history of the land is detailed in *S1/10/11 series 1619-1702*

Lt. Shambles   Two and a half acres included in the sale above.

Shambles Close   Four acres on the west side of the road to Chelmyngton. *GT 1636*

Shamele / Shemele   Half an acre, among four pieces of land in Chelmyngton to which Rose Ingram and her son Richard were admitted. *CR. f.15 6 Hen. VII 1491*. Two acres conveyed by charter to Elizabeth Wulferston, widow. *CR. f.33 21 Hen. VIII 1531*

Sharpells / ?Harpells   One acre among a parcel acquired by Berners from the Parker family. *S1/10/11.18 1827*. Sharpells had one head on the way from Ipswich and the other on the way to Holbrook. *S1/10/11.27 1826*

Shelendclyffe / ?Chelendclyffe   Simply given as the name of a holding for which suit of court was owed; probably in Chelmondiston. *CR. f.19 12 Hen. VII 1497*

Sholande   Matilda de Sholande was assessed 3*s.* in the 1327 Subsidy Returns. *Gr Bk xvi(2)*

Shrubbs   Land lying by a tenement in Holbrook called Whytyngs. *Hol. CR 1670*

le Slade   John Cook owed suit of court. *CR. f.16 7 Hen. VII 1492*

Smart Field   Eight acres sold by Christopher Newham to Samuel Lucas as part of Runtings in 1714. *S1/10/4.9*

Sowthefeld   'Land in Sowthefeld called Bryckeffeld' was among land sold under the terms of Edward Latymer's will. *S1/14/3.3 1544*

Spetmans   *see* Lambards

Spryngswellcroft   A croft and tenement let to John Rede. *CR. f.24 26 Hen. VIII 1535*

Stackyard   A two-acre field sold with other land by Charles Boone to William Berners. *S1/10/3.1 1749*. Listed in the schedule of estate lands; it abutted east on the Barn, south on the road to Woolverstone Hall and north on Bakersfield. *S1/10/4.1 1830*

Strepencroft / ?Stripcroft   Left by John Bakeler to his son Robert. *Will 1481 SROI IC/AA/2/3/1*

Stuttons   George Danyell amerced, owing suit of court. *CR. f.17 10 Hen. VII 1495*

Swamp / Swampy   The boundary of Cages. *S1/10/11.9 1804*. Shown on the Tithe Map as a field on the Freston/Woolverstone boundary. The name is still in use at the present day (1990).

Synthons   Land above Colecroft. *CR. f.14 4 Hen. VII 1489*

Syrigrove / ?Syridrove   Described in John Bakeler's will as five pieces of land in Woolverstone. *1481 SROI IC/AA/2/3/1*

Tailor   *see* Pailor

le Thorne   One of four pieces of land in Chelmondiston granted to Elizabeth Wulferston. It lay · between land of Chelmondiston rectory to the east, Rolfe's land to the west and south, with the Salt Water (river Orwell) to the north. *CR. f. 23 21/22 Hen. VIII 1531* le Thorns   One and a half acres between a tenement of Chelmyngton rectory to the east and land belonging to Rose Ingram to the west, abutting on her land to the north and Dameron's to the south. *CR. f.15 6 Hen. VII 1491*

Threeacres   Six acres of pasture called Threeacres. *CR. f.3 1 Hen. IV 1399*

Tower Shore   The river Orwell shore below Freston Tower, being the western boundary of Bottoms. *S1/10/3.1 1749*

Tracer's Lane Field   Two and a half acres conveyed by Robert Stisted to Robert Brook and later to William Berners in 1755. *HE7:2855 1719*

Tracer / (Grace's)   A messuage and garden, late of Thomas Snell and formerly owned by Robert Tracey, recorded in the marriage settlement of John Goldson. *S1/10/11.4.* 'Grace's' is probably a misreading.

Tracey's Lane   A causeway. *GT 1753*

Truefords   One of several holdings of Sir Thomas Felton; situated between the rectory and land belonging to Knapp, one head on Braky Heath and the other on ffishbane way. *Ct Bk 1711*

Tylers   *see* Petts

Tylhousyerd / Tylkyll   *Oldtylhousyerd* was a pightle conveyed by charter to John Prekytt; it had the Salt Water (i.e. the river Orwell) to the north and was situated between *le Kelne* owned by Thomas Petman, and Prestylbrook. *Newtylhousyerd* was its southern boundary. *CR. f.19 12 Hen. VII 1497.* Tylkyllyerd measuring two acres was conveyed by Thomas Bakeler to John Gardiner of Freston. *S1/14/3.5 1548*

Underwoode   Four acres, part of a quantity of land sold to Thomas Bakeler under Edward Latymer's will. *S1/14/3.3 1544*

le Vant   Granted with land called Boldyrods to John Candysshe. *CR. f.13 1 Hen. VII 1485*

Walsher   Robert Sherman was amerced for cutting coppice wood in Walsher. *CR. f.2 22 Ed. III 1348*

Walton   Thomas Snell admitted to a twelve-acre pasture lying between the way from Dontonstrete to the Salt Water (i.e. the river Orwell) on the east and Arnold's Fen on the west, abutting on the land of Thomas Pitman (Petman) and on

Walton to the south, with the Salt Water to the north. *CR. f.15 6 Hen. VII 1491. See also* Elbury Down

Wardesclose John Warburton admitted to a close and pightle in Peselh below Wardesclose. *CR. f.11 37 Hen. VI 1459*

Warbyltons A tenement and pasture amounting to twelve acres in Wulferston granted to Richard Bryan of Shoteley at a rent of 14s. per annum. *CR. f.28 14 Hen. VIII 1523*

Wardescroft A close adjacent to the King's Highway. *CR. f.2 22 Ed. III 1348*

Wasteland *see* Bottoms

Water Close A five-acre field in Freston abutting to the east on Duckmarshe sold to Henry Pett in 1567. *HE7:2855*

Waterhedge An agreement was recorded to maintain this 'hedge' in the marsh called Duntonffenne adjoining Thomas Goodyng's marshland. Goodyng was a lord of Freston manor, so this was probably a manor boundary. *CR. f.38 33 Eliz. 1591*

Water Shape *or* Willy's Land Four acres, part of land in Woolverstone, Freston and Holbrook sold by Edmund Knapp to Barnaby Burleigh in 1707. *HE7:2855*

Watersheep / Watershepe Thomas Candysshe and Thomas Annyng, clerk, amerced for taking clay without a licence from Watershepe and *le ffoulewater. CR. f.6 11 Hen. IV 1410*

Watersheepes *or* Willislande Land in Freston bequeathed to his wife Elizabeth by Edmund Knapp. *Will PRO 20 Wingfield 1610*

Watyryatte 'Porta aquatica' (i.e. a sluice gate) at *le ffullyngmell. CR. f.27 14 Hen. VIII 1523*

Well Meadow / Corn Meadow / *also* Wolf Meadow A three-acre meadow sold by Philip Catelyn to William Andrewes. *S1/10/3.4 1628.* Named as Wolf (or Wulf) Meadow in the abstract of title. *S1/10/4.4 1774.* The same land is called Corn Meadow in a schedule of Woolverstone estate lands. *S1/10/4.1 1830*

le Wend Thomas Walton amerced for entering the lord's wood and le Wend and cutting down trees. *CR. f.19 12 Hen. VII 1497*

Werryes John Chapman (alias John Felton of Kirkton, Shotley) owed suit of court for this holding. *CR. f.17 10 Hen. VII 1495*

West Croft A three-acre tenement. *CR. f.12 38 Hen. VI 1460*

Westefeld / Westefild / West Field   One arpent granted to Stephen Rolfe in Westefeld. *CR. f.12 38 Hen. VI 1460.* Jonescroft was defined as above Westefild. *CR. f.13 1 Hen. VII 1485.* Richard Snell bequeathed 'my lease of Westefild' to his son John in 1583. *SROI IC/AA/27/252.* West Field, eight acres, appears in the abstract of title concerning Goldson's lands and also in his marriage settlement. *HE7:2855 1684.* A fourteen-year lease was granted to John Gouldson on eight acres in two pieces, one abutting north on the common path to Ipswich and the other south on the same path, known as West Field. *S1/10/4.11 1714.* West Field was the southern boundary of Bridges when purchased by Charles Berners. *S1/10/11.20 1829.* West Field as shown on the Tithe Map has the common way (footpath) on the south, whereas the path lies on the north of the present-day West Field.

Whartelands / Whertelands   Nicholas Snell bequeathed a croft called Whartelands to his son John. *Will SROI IC/AA2/5/90.* George Warry's Whertelands defined the boundary of two acres below Denshwood which were sold under the terms of Edward Latymer's will. *S1/10/14.3 1544.* Whartelands defined the southern head of Lambards when bought by Charles Berners. *S1/10/11.27 1826*

Wheate Meadow   Five and a half acres sold by Christopher Newham to Samuel Lucas as part of Runtings in 1714. *S1/10/4.9*

Whetcroft   Cecilia Birnes recorded as owing suit of court for one piece of land in Whetcroft. *CR. f.13 38 Hen. VI 1461*

Whinney Field   Sold by Philip Catelyn to William Andrewes. *S1/10/3.1 1628.* Listed in a schedule of estate lands. *S1/10/4.1 1830.* Today it is the eastern part of West Field as shown on the 1840 Tithe Map; part was planted with trees in the early 1920s and is still known as Whinney Field Wood.

White House Farm   Stands today at the T-junction of Glebe Lane (Foxhall Lane) with Harkstead Lane, where an old track leads to Grove Farm in Holbrook.

Whiting Street   A 'road' leading from Whiting Street to Dench Wood marked the eastern boundary of Wood Field, three acres, which had a grove of Goldson on the north, a driftway to widow Mason's house on the south and her lands to the west. It was part of Richard Barker's holding in Freston and part of the 226 acres sold in 1707 by Edmond Knapp to Barnaby Burleigh. *HE7:2855*. The name of a road from Woolverstone to Whiting Street in Holbrook and hence to Harkstead. It was the eastern boundary of a three-acre field which was part of the messuage and farm called Sarjeants Heath, sold by Henry Bowle to Thomas Thurston in December 1743. *S1/10/1.2*

Whytynge / Whytyngs John Chychehaugh admitted to land and tenement called Whytyngs in Herkested. *CR. f.14 3 Hen. VII 1488*. John Whytyng was a copyhold tenant in 1460. John Greenleffe was fined for committing waste. *CR. f.26 12 Hen. VIII 1521*. John Greneleffe was named as the free tenant of the holding Whytings in Holbrook. *CR. f.30 18 Hen. VIII 1526*. Land called Shrubbs lying by Whytynge. *Hol. CR 1670*

Willy's Land *see* Water Shape

Wolfreston's Pightle The western boundary of land sold in 1624 under the terms of Hugh Lord's will; the Harkstead to Ipswich highway lay to the south. It formed the eastern boundary of a seven-acre wood, similarly sold. *Suff. Rec. Soc. xxxi 1990*

Wolverston Family name, many versions. The coat of arms is: sable, a fesse wavy between three wolves' heads coupé.

Woolverstone Earliest spellings include: *Uluferestuna* and *Hulferestuna: DB 1086. Wolferston: Feet of Fines 1196. Wolfreston: Copinger, Suff. Rec. & Mss V 1904*

Woolverstone Field Seven and a half acres sold by Christopher Newham to Samuel Lucas in 1714 as part of Runtings. In January 1726 Lucas sold to Knox Ward, who took four and a half acres 'within the Park Pale'. Ralph Ward sold this field with other land to William Berners in 1759. *S1/10/4.9*

Woolverstone Park In 1937 when the Woolverstone estate was offered for sale the Park included Freston Park and comprised 325 acres with 12 acres of garden. When the estate was broken up in 1958 some parkland was sold and turned into farm land, with just 66 acres remaining surrounding the Hall.

Woolverstone Park Field Four and a half acres in the Park taken from Woolverstone Field; included in a schedule of estate lands. *S1/10/4.1 1830*

Wraynecroft A small close abutting on Tracer's Lane towards Ipswich. *GT 1636*

Wrensparke   Fines were recorded for trespass with cows and calves in a wood called Wrensparke. *CR. f.29 16 Hen. VIII 1523*

Wulfelondcroft One messuage, nine buildings, and one croft between Ketylscroft to the south and the King's Highway to the north, abutting partly on manor land; let to John Cobbe for rent, four pigs and suit of court. *CR. f. 21 17 Hen. VII 1502.* Also described, but without a name, in *CR. f.27 14 Hen. VIII 1523.* Possibly named *Hulverscroft* in a seventeenth-century land sale in the *S1/10/11* series.

APPENDIX: PLACE-NAMES IN
DATE ORDER 1348-1635

1348 22 Ed. III	Badylond	Lopymfeld
	Bramacroft	Myddelffen
	Caketon	Newecroft
	Colecroft	Peytenmynes
	Commonfeld	Peselys
	Densshwoode	Sandepettes
	Gristmel	Walsher
	Langstoc	Wardescroft
	Lopham	
1399 1 Hen. IV	Mabbesdonfeld	Threeacres
	Sebbyngcroft	
1402 3 Hen. IV	Bradstok	
	Braham	
1406 7 Hen. IV	Crossespyghtle	Elderobordes
	Crabbe Trees	
1410 11 Hen. IV	le Foulewater	Watersheep (Watershepe)
	Rocketts Grove	
1413 1 Hen. V	le Brodefeldys	Mormanspightle
	Grotesclos	?Netherdonffeld
	Metherdonffeld	Peckecroft
1417 4 Hen. V	Newestrete	
1423 2 Hen. VI	le Pasker	
	le Peschelles	
1459 37 Hen. VI	Commonfeld	
	Harecroft	

1460-61 38 Hen. VI	Caketonheth	Moresheth
	Cukkowyd	Pesfyllyd
	Curtelisdonlands	Pesyllys
	Donton Walton	Westcroft
	Dunton	Westefeld
	ffishbaneway	Whetcroft
	Mershmans	
1485 1 Hen. VII	Boldyrods	Pompards
	Jonescroft	
1488 3 Hen. VII	Bakelers Grove	Pightle in Donton
	Blithes	Podds
	Donnegrove	Poytwynd
	Emryngales	Runtyngs
	Marchamts	Whytyngs
	Newhalle	
1489 4 Hen. VII	le Newholke de Hanburgh	
	?Hammburgh	
	Synthons	
1490 5 Hen. VII	Bramston's Lane	Mowslowe Lane
	le Downe	Podds
	Emmysway	Poytwynd
	Grenecroft in Bradstock	
1491 6 Hen. VII	Arnold's Fen	(?Sowthencroft)
	Birchcroft	Kewescroft
	Chyrchecroft	le Thorns
	Dontonstrete	Longstokheth
	Godmancroft	Oldestreteway
	Howthencroft	Shamele
1492 7 Hen. VII	Bakelerslands	Fletchers
	Bramstons	ffyveacres
	Flechers	
1493 8 Hen. VII	Gretdowne	Reds
	Jirnetts	le Slade
1495 10 Hen. VII	Litildowne	Stuttons
	Purpette	Werryes
1496 11 Hen. VII	Bataylles Grove	
1497 12 Hen. VII	Alcots	Oldtylhousyerd
	Downynnge	le Prestylbrook
	le Kelne	Purpetyd
	Newtylhousyerd	Shelendclyffe
1498 13 Hen. VII	Bakelers	Pynmyll
	Purpets	
1502 17 Hen. VII	Ketylscroft	
	Wulfelondcroft	

1505 20 Hen. VII	Bernecroft	Emmes
	Bradcroft	le ffletchersfeld
	Bramappilion	Foxhole Lane
	Churchwey	Gibbisfen
	Clappers	Piksomes
	Elves Acre	le Poynt
1508 23 Hen. VII	Godfrey's Pitell	Hobbescroft
	Grovetta called Rocketts	
1511 2 Hen. VIII	le Herreyplett	Prynnys
	le Pessels	
1513 4 Hen. VIII	Springswellcroft	
	Litill Lophams	
1521 12 Hen. VIII	Chelendelondys	
	le Lees	
1522-23 14 Hen. VIII	Barnecroft	Pakersmarrshe
	Caketoncroft	Prikytts
	ffullingmell pasture	Warbiltons
	le ffullyngmell	Watyryatte
	le Marsshe	
1524-25 16 Hen. VIII	Bramstonslands	Wrensparke
	Dennysshwode	
1526 18 Hen. VIII	Brygges	
1528-29 19 Hen. VIII	Caketonyerde	Pascarwoode
	Danecroft	Pesselclose
	Melwantwey	
1531 21 Hen. VIII	Holchoncroft	
1590 32 Eliz. I	Affosswalle	ffalegatefeld
	Chekers	Kineslade
	Cherdowne	Kinnelfeld
	Chelendlondes	Langlond
	Estfeld	
1591 33 Eliz. I	Donton ffenne	
1612	Calveton Street	Lt Shambles Farm
	Gt Shambles	
1635	Greneacre	Curtledownefenn

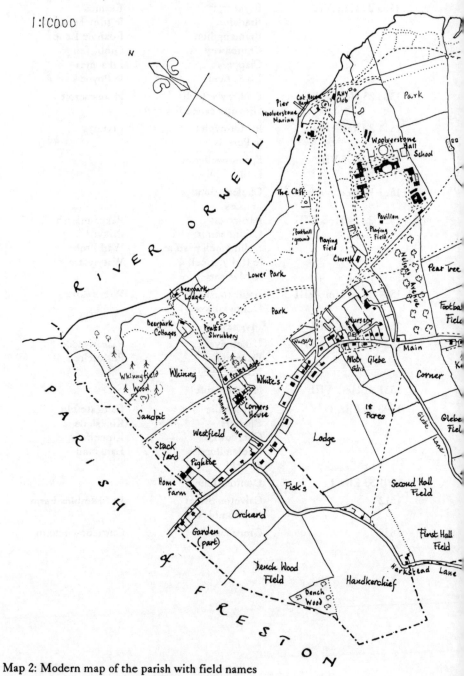

WOOLVERSTONE

FIELD NAMES 1988

1:10000

N

RIVER ORWELL

PARISH

Pier
Cat House
RNV Club
Woolverstone Marina
Park
Woolverstone Hall School
The Cliff
Pavilion
Football ground
Playing Field
Playing Field
Church
Lower Park
Nevill's Avenue
Pear Tree
Deerpark Lodge
Park
Football Field
Deerpark Cottages
Peak's Shrubbery
Nursery
Main
Whinnyfield Wood
Whinny
Peak's Lane
White's
Nursery
Glebe
Corner
Sandpit
Wannings Lane
Corners House
18 Acres
Glebe Lane
Glebe Field
Westfield
Lodge
Stack Yard
Pightle
Home Farm
Fisk's
Second Hall Field
Orchard
Garden (part)
First Hall Field
OF
Dench Wood Field
Dench Wood
Handkerchief
Harkstead Lane
FRESTON

Map 2: Modern map of the parish with field names

50

Park
Cottages

Pony

Vic Hill's

PARISH of CHELMONDISTON

Kennels

Ashcraft

17 acres

Big Field

Bylam
Wood

stackyard

Bylam
Field

Bylam
Lane

house
arm

ISH of HOLBROOK

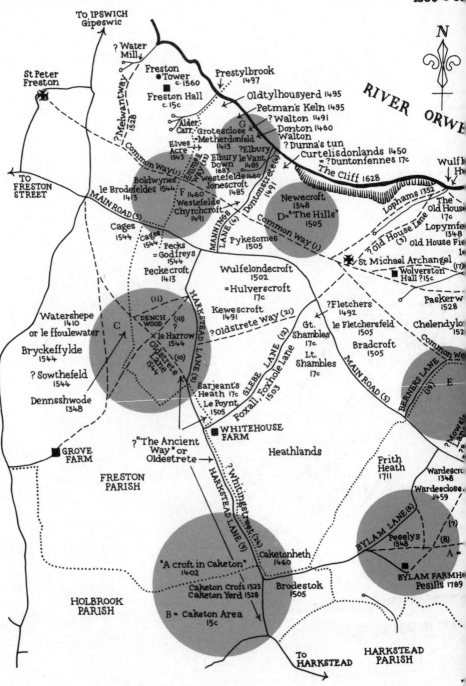

N

To IPSWICH
Gipeswic

? Water
Mill

St Peter
Freston

Freston
Tower
c.1560

Prestylbrook
1497

Freston Hall
c.15c

Oldtylhousyerd 1495
Petman's Keln 1495
?Walton 1491
Donton 1460
Walton
?Dunna's tun
Curtelisdonlands 1450
= ?Duntonfennes 17c

RIVER
ORWE

Wulf

Alder
Carr

Grotesclose
Metherdonfeld

Elves
Acre
1543

?Elbury
Elbury le Vant
1485

Elbury
Down
1683

The Cliff 1628

Lophams 1352

The
Old Hous
17c

Wulf

?Melwantway
1528

Common Way (1)

Boldwynes
le Brodefeldes
1413

F 1460

W.Westefelde 1460
Jonescroft
1485

Westefelde 1485
Chyrchcroft
1491

Newecroft
1348
D="The Hills"
1505

Lopymfe
1348
old House Fie

TO
FRESTON
STREET

MAIN ROAD (5)

Cages
1544

Cages
1544

Pecks
= Godfreys
1544

Peckecroft
1413

Pykesomes
1505

St. Michael Archangel

Wolverston
Hall ?15c

?Old House Lane

Common Way (1)

Wulfelondecroft
1502
= Hulverscroft
17c

Kewescroft
1491

Paskerw
1528

?Fletchers
1492

le Fletchersfeld
1505

Chelendylo
152

Watershepe
1410
or le ffoulewater

Bryckeffylde
1544

? Sowthefeld
1544

Dennsshwode
1348

C

DENCH
WOOD

le Harrow
1544

Oldstrete
Lane
1544

?Oldstrete Way (21)

HARKSTEAD LANE (9)

Gt.
Shambles
17c

Lt.
Shambles
17c

Bradcroft
1505

MAIN ROAD (5)

BERNERS LANE
(19)

E

Common We

Sarjeant's
Heath 17c
Le Poynt
1505

GLEBE LANE (12)

Foxall, Foxhole Lane

Foxall
1503

GROVE
FARM

?"The Ancient
Way" or
Oldestrete →

HARKSTEAD LANE (9)

?Whitingstreet (34)

WHITEHOUSE
FARM

Heathlands

Frith
Heath
1711

Wardescro
1348

Wardesclose
1459

FRESTON
PARISH

BYLAM LANE (6)

Peselys
1348

(7)

(8)

A

HOLBROOK
PARISH

"A croft in Caketon"
1402

Caketonheth
1460

Caketon Croft 1523
Caketon Yerd 1528

B = Caketon Area
15c

Brodestok
1505

BYLAM FARMH
Pesills 1789

TO
HARKSTEAD

HARKSTEAD
PARISH

52

Key:
~ *Shore Line*
— *Present Roads and Lanes*
--- *Footpaths and Tracks*
········ *Parish Boundaries* (1974)
°~ *Springs and Streams*

Present Day Place-names:
Undated in Capitals

Scale: |————————| mile
0   ½

9c
1086

Paskermarsshe
1523

?Runtings
1490
wne 1490 (18)
owne 1490
Shelendcliffe 1497
d   owe Lane 1490
stons Lane
          Shamele
Le Slade   1491
1492   le
     ffulling
     mell 1522
Kineslade
1590
CHELMONDISTON
hyrohe Gate
1488
CH LANE
nscroft
1490
?Newhalle
1485
St Andrew

MAIN ROAD (5)
ON   TO SHOTLEY

Ceolmund's tun 7/9c

PIN MILL

PIN MILL LANE (2)

?Donnegrove
1488

LINGS LANE

AD

53

CHAPTER IV
A 'map' of the Manor: 1350-1600

The landscape in which the manor of Wolverston Hall was functioning during the three hundred years or so covered by the court records was occupied by people living and working in a wide tract of land extending beyond the present parish boundary of Woolverstone deep into Chelmondiston and marginally into other neighbouring parishes. Early (Saxon) farmsteads had grown into hamlets and a scatter of small crofts had been established as land was taken into cultivation from the heaths, woodlands and wastes that fringed the manor.

The landscape would have changed gradually as time passed, but for a long time it included many features absent today; heathlands, downs, meadows, wood pasture with pollarded trees, coppiced woodland providing wood and timber for a variety of purposes, many small enclosed fields, some with cottages, others as separate enclosures and, here and there, a few larger houses ('capital messuages') and, of course, the manor hall and church.

The place-names associated with this long-ago landscape exist only in contemporary documents but they can be used to construct a composite 'picture' of the manor as it may have been during the period 1350-1600. It is presented here in map form. Dates beside the names indicate only that these places were known at those times. There are so many gaps in the records that it is impossible to be more precise about how the manor grew. Some important sites, for instance the mills, sandpits, claypits and manorial rabbit warren, have had to be left out because they could not be located. Before the techniques of surveying and map-making evolved, crofts and closes were located by means of a formula which relied on boundary description. For example: 'a croft lying between land of A to the east and of B to the west, one head abutting on the common way to the south, the other on land of the manor'. Orientation was far from accurate. The manor courts recorded a great deal of information in this jig-saw fashion.

Based on such tenuous clues the manor map provides a very general picture of Woolverstone and Pin Mill before the transition from manor to estate had begun. A few later place-names and some current ones have been included as reference points. The parish boundaries shown, and referred to throughout this book, are those in use prior to the changes of 1974. This map forms the basis for discussion about roads, tracks and other ways (chapter V). In conjunction with the Tithe Map and the modern map of the area, it also acts as a framework for ideas about ancient settlements, patterns and changes in land-use advanced in chapter VI.

It should be remembered that the Orwell foreshore has been, and still is, subject to considerable erosion, so riverside sites must have occupied more space than suggested by the map, which was drawn using the mean high water line on the 1975 OS map. For the same reason, some of the riverside paths will have been washed away. Parts of the lands once occupied by the manor will therefore now lie concealed beneath mudflats.

The following key explains the numbering used for the roads and tracks on the map and in the text. It also indicates by letters some of the sites discussed in chapter VI; these are shaded on the map.

Key: Roads and tracks

1 common way
2 Pin Mill Lane
3 way to river via the back drive to the Hall and footpath ?Old House Lane
4 Mannings Lane (Love Lane) = Dontonstrete, Donslon Street
5 main road from Ipswich to Shotley
= King's Highway = Gippeswic to Fishbane road or way
6 Bylam Lane
7/8 tracks and paths to Bylam Farm (once Pesills or Peselys)
9 Harkstead Lane
10 former lanes into Dench Wood from Harkstead Lane
11 another path into Dench Wood
12 Glebe Lane = Foxall or Foxhole Lane
13 ways from the common way to Pin Mill
14 Church Lane, Chelmondiston
15 Richardson's Lane and track to the shore and Pin Mill
16 damp track from the common way to Pin Mill
17 a more direct route to Pin Mill over the cricket ground
18 shore path from the Tileyard to Pin Mill
19 Berners Lane (also = Love Lane)
20 Mowslowe or Bramston's Lane
21 ?Oldstreteway
22 ?Newestrete
23 ?Emmesway
24 ?Whiting Street

Key to shaded areas

A Peselys (Pesills, Bylam Farm)
B Caketon
C Dennsshwoode
D ?Bronze Age burial mounds (Park Field)
E ?Estfeld
F Westfeld (West Field, Sandpit/Whinney Fields)
G Donton/Walton area

CHAPTER V
Roads and tracks

Continuity with the past is to be found most easily not through the names of places but in the network of roads, lanes, tracks and footpaths which, over the years, have connected manor and parish with the church, the Hall and neighbouring places including the ports and markets of Ipswich and Shotley. And so, although the numerous place-names in use by the manor's inhabitants are now unrecognisable, the routes that people used as they went about their everyday lives are either still in use or can be traced as tracks or footpaths even though their old names have been lost or changed.

These routes had their origin in the distant past. Indeed, it seems possible that when the tenants of Wolverston Hall went out into the fields or elsewhere to work, and when they walked to church or to the manor court, some of the ways they used could have been in existence in Roman times, or even earlier. There is, as yet, no evidence to indicate when and by whom these ancient ways were made, but the old ways do not necessarily disappear, especially when they continue to provide convenient routes.

Since they were effectively the manor's lifelines, they form the basic structure into which the manor names have been placed to produce the accompanying map. Figures in brackets in the text match those beside the ways, lanes and paths shown on the map. Some present-day names are included.

It is important to remember that these land-based routes were augmented from time immemorial by waterways: the tidal river Orwell has always been accessible from numerous hards and landing places all along the northerly border of the Shotley Peninsula. They have no place in this survey simply because they were not to be found in the sources used.

The oldest ways

Initially these served Anglo-Saxon and any earlier settlements. Later they focused on the church. Present-day footpaths follow the same routes. The most important is a markedly straight-through route (1). It can be followed north-west from the church across field paths towards Freston and thence to Wherstead and Ipswich. In the opposite direction it leads over fields and a track (Chelmondiston Church Lane) to the church there. It probably continued further eastward along Hollow Lane, across Pin Mill Lane and away towards Shotley.

For almost the whole length of its course between Chelmondiston and Freston the footpath lies on level dry ground above the spring line. There

are many references to it in manorial and other records as the common way
(1). That it may have been a track linking Roman sites has been suggested,
though so far no supporting evidence has been unearthed. Since it links
the heads of three steep valleys that lead to sheltered open ground beside
the river Orwell its origins could well have been associated with farmsteads
established in these fertile valley bottoms even before the advent of
Anglo-Saxon settlers.

In the late Saxon period these evolved into hamlets that later became
Chelmondiston and Woolverstone. A third hamlet, referred to in the early
sixteenth century as Dunton in Walton, failed to develop. Walton itself
may also have been a lost settlement site.

The ways from these early settlements to the common way that linked
them and led further afield appear to have become, respectively, Pin Mill
Lane (2); an unnamed footpath through Woolverstone Park, possibly the
lost Old House Lane (3); and the rough northernmost section of Mannings
Lane (4). This last was once known as Dontonstrete or Donslon Street.
The present winding main road (5) is more or less parallel to the common
way footpath. Its old names – the King's Highway, the Gyppeswic to
ffyschbane road and le Portweye in the thirteenth century – provide no
clues as to its origin.

Many routes familiar to the medieval manor tenants were work ways;
for instance, ways to their grazing grounds. Seven places were named at the
1348 manor court as 'the lord's pasture'. They were used as common
grazing land: Peselys, Caketon, Densshwoode, Langstok, Commonfeld,
Badylond and Myddelffen (Plate 1).

Peselys became the 'manor or farm' called Pesills in the sixteenth
century. It was called Bickmore's when Charles Berners bought it in 1789.
Today it is Bylam Farm, occupying some 90 acres, almost all in
Chelmondiston. Present-day Bylam Lane (6) and footpaths (7, 8) that
converge near the modern farm buildings must surely have originated as
tracks along which the manor tenants drove their sheep and other animals
to graze at Peselys nearly 600 years ago.

Caketon occupied land at the junction of the three parishes of
Woolverstone, Freston and Harkstead where Bylam Lane (6) meets
Harkstead Lane (9). The forerunners of these lanes would have provided
easy access to the manor's scattered crofts. There were 40 acres of
heathland at Caketonheth in 1460 and in 1490 a 28-acre holding called
Caketon croft.

Dennsshwoode must have been much larger than the present Dench
Wood; the unexpected curve in Harkstead Lane (9) could well have
marked its eastern boundary. It probably extended over the present Dench
Wood Field and the field in Freston called Great Dents (Tithe Map 1839).
Since it was used for grazing and for pannage, it must have been wood-

pasture. Old routes to it from the main road probably followed Harkstead Lane and thence into the pasture by unnamed lanes (10) shown on the Tithe Map. These coincide with tracks shown on nineteenth-century OS maps. Another path (11) leading to Dench Wood is shown on the County Council's footpath map. None of these is discernible in the fields today.

Longstok was a long stretch of heathland, between Harkstead Lane (9) and Glebe Lane (12), with access from the forerunners of these lanes.

Badylond has not been identified.

Myddelfenn, being marshy or wet grazing land, is also difficult to place, as several sites would fit this description. The most likely seems to be a fen in Dunton Walton called Dunton Fennes (1419). If so, it would have been reached by Dontonstrete, now Mannings Lane (4). Evidence from associated place-names supports this choice.

There are no clues to suggest where Commonfeld was.

Ways to Pin Mill

In addition to Pin Mill Lane (2) there are two footpaths that may have connected it to the common way: both still exist. One (13) leaves the common way just before the present Chelmondiston Church Lane (14) to join a rough track to the riverside. This track was part of a route from the main road to Pin Mill until it was closed by Charles Berners in 1807 after a dispute about a right of way. The southern end of this former 'road' still exists as Richardson's Lane (15).

The other path (16) leaves the common way just behind the site of the old manor house (now the stable block). It leads down to a damp valley to the riverside and so to Pin Mill. A drier and more direct route (17), which is shown on the Tithe Map, passed between the site of the old manor house and the Berners' new Hall. No doubt it was closed when the Berners' private cricket ground was laid over it.

Tileyard and mill

A path along the shore (18) connects the site of the old tileyard, beside the Freston parish boundary, with Pin Mill. Tile making was in operation at this site in the fifteenth century (Plate 18). The field on its western side (in Freston) was named on the Freston Tithe Map as Landing Field, so tiles may have been delivered by water as well as by any of the tracks leading from the riverside to the main road.

There are several early references to grist mills in Woolverstone, but no clues as to their whereabouts until a mortgage of 1723 describes a mill in Woolverstone as lying between the Old House and The Cliff, and therefore reached by Old House Lane (3). A small stream runs into the river in this area.

Sites where clay, gravel and sand were extracted are referred to, but it has not been possible to locate them.

Ways to the church and manor court

Most of the old paths already described focus on St Michael's church. If this church stands on the site of that listed in the Domesday Survey, then these paths are at least a thousand years old.

Another way to the church was Foxall Lane (12), which became Glebe Lane after an exchange of glebe land in the eighteenth century. In the seventeenth century an extension of this lane once led past the rectory straight to the church (12a).

The manor house leased by William Berners before moving into his new hall was a brick-clad timber-framed building (Plate 19). The slim red Tudor bricks can still be seen in the walls of the stable block erected in its place. The common way and its several tributaries all provided access to this manor house where, no doubt, courts were held.

Lost lanes

Old House Lane led to an old house by the river. This house may have been the 'capital messuage' called Lophams. References to the name Lophams are included in chapter III. The house itself and its possible connections with the Cat House are discussed in the appendix. In the eighteenth century, Old House Lane appears to have become a private lane from the King's Highway to Knox Ward's riverside malting office. Its course is now hidden within Woolverstone Park, possibly in part beneath the back drive (3) to the Hall, from which it would have continued on the line of the present footpath to the area now occupied by the Royal Harwich Yacht Club.

Berners Lane (19), now just a farm track, lies on part of the parish boundary with Chelmondiston. It connects the main road with the common way (1), which it joins at right-angles. The latter then edges round a large level arable field that is almost certainly the successor of the Estfeld referred to in the manor records of 1590. The track then dips sharply as it passes Page's Common. In 1490 there was a lane in this area called Mowslowe Lane or Bramston's Lane (20). This was probably the continuation of present-day Richardson's Lane, leading to Pin Mill as described above (13). How much of this route was called Berners Lane is not known: when the right of way over the stretch (13) was in dispute in 1807, a plan (Plate 7) simply labels present-day Berners and Richardson's Lanes as 'First Lane' and 'Second Lane'.[26]

Mary's Lane appears to have been a turning off Old House Lane and is therefore lost within Woolverstone Park.

Tracey's Lane was referred to in relation to land 'late of Robert Tracey'. It led towards Ipswich and was somewhere in the north-west of Woolverstone; it may have been a name used for part of the common way.

Emmesway (23) is mentioned only once, at a court held in 1490. It was described as leading north off the common way, presumably to the holding called Emmes or Emmscroft. The ownership, although not the exact location, of this holding is well documented. It, too, was in the north-west part of Woolverstone lying partly in Freston. A farm track leading off the old common way (1) in the presumed direction of Emmes existed until it was ploughed up in the 1980s.

Stretes and Roman roads?

Six 'strete' or Street names have been found in the documents studied for this survey. Five were clearly in Woolverstone: Whiting Street, Dontonstrete (Donslon Street), Newestrete, Oldstreteway and Oldstrete Lane.

The sixth, Calveton Street, was almost certainly associated with the present-day Calton on the Shotley/Chelmondiston parish boundary; its history is outside the scope of this book. The name 'Street' today generally refers to a straggling hamlet. All the parishes around Woolverstone (Freston, Chelmondiston, Shotley, Holbrook, Stutton) still have streets of this type, although the local authority seems bent on naming them Main Roads. Woolverstone lacks a 'Street' in this sense. Whiting Street was quoted as a boundary in 1827, though not described sufficiently clearly to identify it. In 1743 a 'road' led from Whiting Street to Dench Wood. At that time the name may have referred to a straggling hamlet which has left no trace. Its earlier association with a postulated Roman track is discussed below.

Donslon Street was almost certainly called Dontonstrete in 1491. It has been identified with present-day Mannings Lane (4). This lane becomes steep and narrow very soon after crossing the common way footpath (1), having a high bank on its westerly side most of the way down to the river Orwell, and sloping wet land on the east. It is difficult to imagine a Street-type hamlet at the river end, unless it occupied level ground since lost by erosion. The southerly stretch of Mannings Lane seems a more suitable site for a straggle of dwellings, sited close to the common-way crossing, in the area now occupied by a small group of former estate cottages. No specific evidence has been found to support this suggestion.

Newestrete, mentioned once only, briefly, in a 1417 court record, is impossible to locate.

Oldstreteway (the way to Oldstrete) appears to have linked Foxall Lane, now Glebe Lane (12), with Harkstead Lane (9), probably crossing Longstokheth. Described as Oldstrete Lane in 1544, it went 'from Woolverstone towards Harkstead'. Another sixteenth-century document relating to Mere Field in Freston refers to 'an ancient way' to Dench Wood. In the same collection of documents a lengthy evidence of title relating to fields including Mere Field mentions 'a road leading from Whiting to Dench Wood'.

Considering these, admittedly slight, clues in relation to a straight stretch of the Woolverstone/Holbrook parish boundary, it is possible to visualise, on the present 6-inch OS map (TM 13 NE), a Roman road or track running north-east from Bylam Cottages to White House Farm and straight on, leaving the parish boundary to pass through Dench Wood (then much larger than it is today), and so on into Freston parish. This, perhaps, was part of the 'ancient way'. Whether or not Whiting Street was ever a straggling hamlet, the name might point back to a time when it formed part of this same 'way'.

An eighteenth-century abstract of title included an ambiguous reference to a road 'from Woolverstone to Whiting Street and thence to Harkstead'. The only existing road that fits this description is a continuation of Harkstead Lane (9) southwards beyond its junction with Bylam Lane (6) just past Bylam Cottages. It crosses a corner of Holbrook parish where it becomes the long straight 'Ipswich Road'. This route could be seen as the southerly continuation of the postulated 'ancient way' or Oldstrete. It is remarkably straight, in striking contrast with the meandering lanes it connects.

Arrows on the manor map show this section of the 'ancient way'. Where did it start and end? Ipswich Road, Harkstead, joins Harkstead Street at right-angles; from there, a footpath continues the line to the shore of the river Stour, giving access to the sea and thence to the Roman settlement at Walton (Felixstowe).

In Freston parish, crop marks on an aerial photograph appear to continue the line towards Valley Farm in Wherstead. From there, lanes and footpaths indicate how the line may have crossed Belstead parish to connect with the Roman road (A1214) at Copdock, thus giving access to local markets in Colchester and Coddenham.

The idea of such a link road is attractive, but much more research is needed to give this tentative suggestion substance. There is no doubt that there were Romano-British farms on the Shotley Peninsula: twenty sites (not necessarily farms) are shown on John Newman's 1992 map of Romano-British settlements in S E Suffolk. Roads or well-surfaced trackways would have been needed for transporting farm produce, for access to the Orwell and Stour estuaries and for communication generally.

Attempting to trace them now, nearly two thousand years later, presents formidable problems. Shadowy marks on aerial photographs may suggest the existence of former lanes or tracks, but give no indication of their age. Parish boundaries, as they appear on early OS maps, may follow the route of roads or tracks – including those of Roman origin – still in existence when parishes were being delineated. But without supporting evidence, parish boundaries provide only limited guidance.

EXPLORING THE PAST THROUGH PLACE-NAMES

Evidence to be deduced from place-names that include the element *-strete* has, so far, only yielded the best of a meagre collection of clues about the Roman ways that once ran through and beyond Woolverstone. At present, placing these 'stretes' on a map can be little more than guesswork. Tracing them more precisely provides a challenging subject for future research.

CHAPTER VI
Place-names, settlements and landscape

In attempting to reconstruct past landscapes and to understand how and why they changed with time, place-names can be very useful, although their value is limited by the availability of documentary sources. Where an abundant supply of early place-names can be allied with the results of aerial photography and archaeological fieldwork they are capable of throwing light on developments that range far back into prehistoric times.

This chapter shows how, by applying this combined approach to specific areas once governed by the manor of Wolverston Hall, new insights into past patterns of settlement and land-use can be discerned. Then, after a review of post-manorial development, it concludes with a brief comment on current and possible future place-names in Woolverstone.

Saxon origins
In seeking to discover the origins of Woolverstone, place-names alone are sufficient to point to a Saxon presence, for, with few exceptions, their roots are Old English. The Anglo-Saxon personal names *Dunna, Wulfhere* and *Ceolmund,* from which *Dunton, Wolferston* and *Ceolmundeston* may be derived suggest that during the Middle Saxon period (the seventh to ninth centuries) there were Saxon farmsteads along the Orwell shore between the Freston/Woolverstone boundary and Pin Mill (Chelmondiston). The people who settled here may have been immigrants or they may have moved down the river from Ipswich, already a flourishing town at that time.

No place-names directly derived from the British language have been discovered but this does not mean that the Anglo-Saxons moved into uninhabited land. Presumably they would have given their own names to places in their new territory, perhaps because they did not understand or could not pronounce existing names, or perhaps they simply preferred their own.

Development from these Saxon farmsteads to the widespread pattern of crofts and closes known to exist in the fifteenth and sixteenth centuries would have been a slow process. The original settlements by the river spread into the neighbouring valleys to exploit the good pasture and meadowland nearby and the light well-drained soils on higher level ground to the south, suitable for arable crops. In 1086 the Domesday Survey reported enough (arable) land for two and a half plough teams in Woolverstone (*Uluferestuna*).

Later, as the population increased, land was taken into cultivation from the heaths, woodland and wastes that fringed the manor. Place-names confirm the existence of a concentration of crofts and closes and other features in the Donton/Walton area (shaded G on the manor map) in the fifteenth and sixteenth centuries. The fenns (low-lying pastures) in this area were fourteenth-century common grazing grounds. Two similar groups of places existed south-west of Pin Mill extending into the area now occupied by Bylam Farm (shaded A and E on the manor map).

A corresponding 'hamlet' has not been traced in the neighbourhood of the Saxon farmstead of *Wulfhere*, perhaps because this riverside site had already been deserted before 1348 (the date of the first surviving manor court record). Presumably by then the descendants of *Wulfhere* were living further inland.

It seems unlikely that the Middle Saxon settlers were the first inhabitants of their territory. An extensive survey carried out in the Deben Valley area of south-east Suffolk between 1983 and 1988 by John Newman as part of the East Anglian Kingdom Survey[27] has shown that small scattered settlements existed there from the Bronze Age right through Anglo-Saxon times. So far, only small portions of such a pattern have been found in the Shotley Peninsula. Already, there are strong hints of dispersed prehistoric and Romano-British settlements in the area, but evidence of Early Saxon habitation – which might be expected – is completely lacking. John Newman suggests that this may represent some form of Romano-British survival in a world experiencing increasing dominance by newcomers in the Middle Saxon period. Unfortunately this is a proposition difficult to confirm purely by archaeological methods, and place-names studies have little to contribute, at least in this Woolverstone/ Chelmondiston area.

The existence of Woolverstone Park and the prohibition of metal detectors in some parts of the parish have greatly limited opportunities for finding traces of pre-Saxon habitation, but three interesting sites have been explored in a series of backward steps, by combining place-names with results of aerial survey and field-walking. The evidence is thin and the arguments speculative but the findings may prove a useful basis for further discussion and investigation.

A *Bronze Age site?*
Park Field and Lower Park Field in Woolverstone (see modern map) have been arable fields, ploughed regularly, for the past thirty years. Previously they were parkland for some two hundred years, undisturbed except when the carriage drive was made and estate sewers were laid. Earlier, the area had been arable land, part of the manor's demesne. It was first sold in 1628. No field-names that might have been associated with the land before that date have been found. On the manor map the area therefore appears blank

(shaded area D). Large amounts of broken red tiles were collected recently from the surface of Park Field. They are similar to fragments found at the nearby site of a medieval tileyard, prompting the suggestion that they might have been the roofs of buildings.

Indeed, perhaps this was the site of a lost Woolverstone hamlet. Belief persists locally that 'the old village was wiped out by the plague', but facts are lacking. In 1348 there were at least thirty-five households in the manor; how these people were affected by the Black Death that arrived the following year is impossible to ascertain because the membrane recording the post-plague courts, held in 1349 and 1351, is so worn that it is illegible. Nor can the progress of recovery be traced, for there is a gap in the manor record until 1399 when twenty-two men swore fealty to their new lord, Alice, widow of Roger Wolferston. No good explanation for the surface scatter of tile fragments has been suggested. Their place in the sequence of land-use in this area might be clarified if they could be dated.

Other finds collected on several field-walking expeditions have much earlier origins; worked flints, flint flakes and a few pottery shards suggest the presence of farmers in the Late Neolithic to Early Bronze Age periods.[28]

An aerial photograph of Park Field and Lower Park Field taken during the summer drought of 1975[29(a)] shows a network of crop marks (Plate 15). The pipelines and inspection covers of the estate sewerage system are clearly visible superimposed on the marks of buried features relating to indeterminable times in the past.

Interpretation of these marks is far from simple. The photographic print held in the University of Cambridge Library of Air Photographs is annotated 'polygonal networks'. These are geological features which occur in sandy soil as the result of freezing during glaciation and subsequent thawing. First, freezing produced a network of ice-wedge polygons. These, when the ice melted, left voids into which adjacent sediments collapsed, thus preserving the polygonal pattern. These networks give rise to crop marks (i.e., patches lighter or darker than the surrounding areas) which in aerial photographs can look like those produced by small ditched fields. The crop marks in Park Field therefore remain ambiguous until skilled appreciation can be made.

Another photograph[29(b)] gives a bird's-eye view of two low, tree-covered mounds that stand in Lower Park Field near the former carriage drive (Plate 16). The trees were probably planted as landscape features when the land was emparked or, more likely, when the drive was made in the mid-nineteenth century; but there is no doubt that the mounds themselves pre-date the Park. On the manor map, in the north-west corner of the area, there is a croft with an untypical double-barrelled name: *New Croft or The Hills*, which name persisted until 1830 when it was given as *The Hills alias*

New Croft. It is impossible to determine how long the croft had been there when it was first mentioned as *Newecroft* in the manor record of 1348. Although it was then called 'new' it could well have been so called long before. In Suffolk, and almost everywhere else, 'new' tends to be an imprecise term unrelated to actual age. It therefore seems reasonable to assume that the croft acquired its alternative name *The Hills* from the nearby mounds which must have been a prominent feature in the landscape. Perhaps they are Bronze Age burial mounds?

The Manor's Great Fields: Estfeld and Westefeld

These two fields were more or less equidistant from the old manor house and church (see manor map). Both lay next to straight stretches of Woolverstone's parish boundary, both were bounded by the King's Highway (5) and both had an ancient lane (Mowslowe Lane (20) and Duntonstrete (4) respectively) as a third boundary. Estfeld's name was lost after the sixteenth century; the name Westfield has survived. The names imply that at some stage of the manor's history these were Great Fields; common or 'open' arable fields. Originally they would have been farmed communally in strips, but this system had already been abandoned by the mid-fourteenth century. Only one reference to strips as such ('a holding in seven strips') occurs in the court roll, but field-names that include the elements *acre*, *land* and *lond* are significant. There are fifteenth-century references to grants of land 'in the field' and 'in the commonfeld', which indicate that enclosure was then in progress, but how long since it had begun is impossible to tell.

Complex crop patterns are visible on 1975 aerial photographs of both areas. Their meaning is far from clear but some of the more recent changes in land-use can be traced through field-names, and fieldwork is beginning to provide clues about earlier times. In combination, this collection of evidence suggests possible causes of at least some of the enigmatic crop marks.

Estfeld land uses: sheep farming?

Estfeld lay in an area now occupied by a large arable field in Chelmondiston just east of the Woolverstone parish boundary. Three 'field-names' are now used to define different cropping areas in it. One of these, Page's Common, is a reference to a nearby piece of Common on the east of the boundary lane (15). Ditches associated with the three fields, obliterated when the hedges were removed, may account for some of the crop marks visible in aerial photographs taken in 1975 and 1977 (Plates 10, 12 and 13).[30, 31]

The Chelmondiston Tithe Map[32] drawn up in 1839 shows ten fields in the area including Barn Field and Barn Meadow. When the building was removed and hedges grubbed out the disturbed soil would have been liable to produce crop marks in cereal crops during drought conditions. A 1590 charter describes Estfeld as 'otherwise Falegatefeld', indicating that the former Great Field was still remembered by a name originating from when all or part of it was used for sheep farming. (The fulling mill was barely half a mile away at Pin Mill.)

The apparent absence of names of crops and closes suggests that much of Estfeld may have remained open for a long period. If so, it would appear unlikely that the crop marks relate to medieval land use.

The large modern field has not yet been explored systematically by field-walking or metal-detecting, but in adjacent fields these techniques have yielded finds from Romano-British and Saxon periods, as well as a scatter of medieval pottery shards. It seems, therefore, that Page's Common Field and its environs have been farmed either continuously or intermittently for nearly two thousand years. One of the settlements may have developed from Ceolmund's initial Saxon farmstead.

Westefeld – and a lost hamlet?

Today the area once occupied by the manor's western open field, Westefeld, is again a large tract of arable land, bisected now as then by the common way footpath (1). The name West Field is still in use, although it now refers only to the south-east corner of the area. The other current names are topographical; Stackyard between West Field and Home Farm's yards and, to the north of the common way footpath, Sandpit Field (with a disused sandpit in one corner) and Whinney Field. These last two border on Whinney Field Wood, which contains a mixture of conifers and deciduous trees planted in the nineteenth century to link two alder carrs.

The Woolverstone Tithe Map shows West Field to have been an irregularly shaped piece of land north of the common way footpath, lying between two alder carrs and stretching as far as Last's Meadow by the river. The whole of the southerly area was then named Hog's Trough; Hobbscroft was its name in 1508.

The manor map presents a very different landscape. In the fifteenth and sixteenth centuries the name West Field was used to refer to land on either side of the common way. Parts of it had been enclosed to form Hobbscroft and a holding called Brygges (1526), both lying to the south of the common way. To the north lay Emmes (1505), 'three closes lying together'; Chyrchecroft (1491), 'beside the common way'; and Jonescroft (1485), 'lying above West Field'.

An excellent photograph of the Westefeld/West Field area (Plate 9), taken during the aerial survey in 1975, shows crop marks in present-day Sandpit Field.[34] They may relate to the manor's crofts and closes of the fifteenth and sixteenth centuries. They may also indicate the margins of an earlier settlement, located in territory bordering the river and extending from the Prestyl brook (1497), which forms the Freston/Woolverstone boundary, to the western end of The Cliff. The ancient Dontonstrete (4) would have provided access from the common way to this pleasantly sheltered area, variously referred to as Donton or Dunton in Walton. Perhaps it was once a hamlet, grown from the postulated Saxon farmstead *Dunna's tún*, which failed to survive beyond the sixteenth century. Interesting places associated with it included several fens used as common grazing ground from 1348, le Vant (1485), the old tileyard and Petman's keln (1497), and Elbury Down; Elbury may have been an ancient fortified or defensible site. The meanings and possible derivations of these place-names are discussed further in the Appendix. Unfortunately almost all of this intriguing area is inaccessible in parkland or covered by woodland used as a game preserve, so neither air-borne camera nor archaeological fieldwork can be used to throw more light on it.

A nucleated village?

Archaeological finds from the spoil and disturbed ground at several sites south and east of Woolverstone church, when a new sewage pipeline was laid through the Park in 1991, included pottery sherds dateable from the ninth through to the fourteenth century (SMR WLV 012). These and earlier finds of medieval pottery sherds in the same area suggest that a Saxon settlement associated with the pre-Domesday church developed as a nucleated village which remained there while the open field system of farming continued. This would have been a three-field system if Lopymfeld was cultivated in addition to Estfeld and Westefeld. Subsequent enclosure of these fields, traceable in the manor records, seems to have led to some movement away from this central area, as reflected in the field-names of the period. This postulated phase has left no visible signs in the landscape.

Development 1600-1840 – a lost landscape

It has proved impossible to construct a map relevant to any phase of the transitional period during which the manor became part of the much larger Woolverstone estate. From 1600 onwards the manor courts rarely mentioned holdings by name. Only ten of the early place-names appear in records between 1600 and 1791, when the manor ceased to exist. The only new names were Busshy Close (1658); The Purlieu (1682); and two heaths, Braky Heath and Frith Heath (both 1711). Generally, holdings were referred to by the tenants' names, a system which gives no clue as to their whereabouts. Other sources used for this survey were equally uninformative about where Woolverstone's inhabitants lived and worked between 1600 and 1840.

The land transactions of the seventeenth and eighteenth centuries, which eventually culminated in the break-up of the manor, resulted in even greater uncertainty over field-names. Some of the land passed to families long- resident in the manor who must have known the fields by their old names. However, large tracts of land were sold to wealthy townspeople new to country life. To them – and to their lawyers – a field was just a field, almost always defined by the names of past or contemporary owners and occupiers. It is not surprising that documents drawn up to provide evidence, or abstract, of title were subject to mistakes over dates and names. Ownership, and hence the right to sell, often had to be traced back through a bewildering series of family relationships recorded in barely legible papers and deeds.

William Berners bought his first land in Woolverstone in 1749; sixty acres comprising thirteen named fields. It seems that these same fields with almost identical names had already been bought by John Tyssen in 1720, a fact which only came to light in 1773 when the Chancery Court permitted William Berners to purchase what then amounted to the entire Woolverstone estate.

The lack of topographical place-names and the difficulty of locating those described by means of personal names were not the only difficulties encountered in trying to follow changes in the field and settlement patterns in Woolverstone during the course of the seventeenth and eighteenth centuries.

The main obstacle was the existence of the Park. Emparking had begun before William Berners' time. Knox Ward took four and a half acres 'within his park pale' in 1726, which implies that a park was already then in existence. Its extent is not known; a plan of the estate as it was in 1720 was originally annexed to the relevant deed, but is no longer attached and so far has not been traced.

William Berners enclosed three hundred acres soon after he acquired the estate. Hodskinson's map,[35] published some ten years later, shows the extent of the Park in 1783 (Plate 5). William's son Charles continued to take in land until the Park, at nearly four hundred acres, covered almost half the parish. An archive of 1835[36] lists many field-names which were in use when various parcels of land were bought, but by that time most of these fields had long since vanished within the Park and others elsewhere in the parish had acquired different names, as the 1840 Tithe Map shows.

Landscape clearance. A lost village?
The story[14] that 'the Berners destroyed the old village to make the Park', pulling down all the old houses and moving people into new estate cottages, is manifestly untrue. Dates still just discernible on these cottages prove that they were built some hundred years after the Park had been enclosed.

Hodskinson's map shows not only the extent of the Park in 1783 but also the layout of the village of Woolverstone. Clearly most of the villagers at that time were already living in cottages outside the Park. The estate papers make no reference to wholesale clearance. All the available evidence suggests that few people had been living in the area taken into the Park. Why and when they settled along the main road remains a mystery.

Changes within the Park

Certainly some buildings known to have been in the park area disappeared. The fate of some of them, notably the old manor and the old rectory, is well known, whereas that of others provides scope for speculation.

The old manor house was pulled down on the orders of William Berners after he moved into the new Hall. An undated pencil sketch made before the demolition began is now in the Fitch Collection held by the Suffolk Record Office in Ipswich.[37]

The old rectory near the church was left empty after the living was amalgamated with that of Erwarton. The building became increasingly dilapidated, until in 1819 Charles Berners obtained a faculty from the Bishop of Norwich allowing him to have it pulled down. Glebe land on which the rectory stood was exchanged for land outside the Park pale. The plan[38] relating to this transaction shows the old rectory occupying the site of the model dairy, built some fifty years later.

Other lost places

A mill house, a malting office, sundry outbuildings, a mysterious Old House and perhaps one or two cottages existed in the seventeenth century beside the river to the east of The Cliff.[39] There was also 'a capital messuage called Lophams' in the area; this was sold by the then lord of the manor in 1628 and later bought as part of William Berners' first land acquisition in Woolverstone.[40]

By 1840 not one of these buildings was still standing. Whether they were pulled down or had already fallen into decay by the time the area was enclosed we shall never know. Lath and plaster cottages and even timber-framed buildings will collapse if not kept in good repair. The long years during which the ownership of the Woolverstone estate was being argued in the Chancery Court were hardly conducive to good maintenance.

Lophams alias The Old House?

The name *Lophams* implies that the messuage belonged originally to the de Lopham family. They were the patrons of Woolverstone church from 1086 until at least 1349, when William de Lopham presented Thomas Orger to the living.[41] A family with this surname originated in Norfolk: the villages of North and South Lopham lie just north of the Suffolk border. The name *Lophams* disappeared from the Woolverstone records in the eighteenth century; at about the same time there are references to The Old House, situated apparently in the same area as Lophams east of The Cliff. Old House Lane and Old House Field were associated with it. Perhaps by then the ancient Lophams was regarded simply as an old nameless house. It was probably beyond repair when the Park was created.

A chantry chapel?

If it is true that there was once a chantry chapel where The Cat House[14] now stands, it may have been built for one of the de Lophams before the Wolferstons became lords of the manor in 1419. It would have been conveniently near to their house. There is no record of a chantry in Woolverstone in the sixteenth century. Whether it existed before then remains an unanswered question.

Lost places outside the Park

The group of Baptists[42] formed in Woolverstone in 1757 used a cottage in the village as their Meeting House and the 'old' Cat House cottage in the Park for baptism services which required total immersion in the nearby river. The estate claimed The Cat House cottage after William Berners' lawyers discovered that the Baptists had no title to it. They then founded a new church in Ipswich at Stoke Green. The old Meeting House did not survive long enough to appear on the Tithe Map, but Meeting House Field shows where it stood and Meeting House Yard appears on a map of the Leggatt estate.[43] Even these place-names have since been lost.

The Ball Inn beside the main Ipswich-Shotley road lasted long enough to be recorded on the Tithe Map, but the Hare and Hounds had already disappeared and not so much as a field-name now recalls it.

Development 1840-1990

In 1840, for the first time, the whole of Woolverstone parish was placed on record when the Tithe Map was published, accompanied by a comprehensive list of owners and occupiers of every piece of land and every building within the parish. This map shows a landscape of small fields of precisely measured acreage, a few surviving meadows, some ancient alder carr, a scatter of cottages and, in the Park, the isolated church and the Hall with its stable block, outbuildings and gardens. The only houses in the Park were the head gardener's newly built thatched cottage and the Cat House. Details of how each place listed in the tithe apportionment has changed between 1840 and the present day (1990) have already been presented in chapter II.

The landscape of 1840 was one of great contrast. The spacious Park covered almost all the northerly half of the parish, leaving the remainder to be farmed in a multitude of small fields. No great changes occurred until the estate was dispersed in 1958.

Since then a very different landscape has evolved. Large tracts of former parkland have reverted to arable cropping in new fields both east and west of the remaining Park. Confusingly, all are called Park Field. The little estate fields have lost their dividing hedges and been amalgamated to accommodate modern farm machinery. An aerial survey commissioned by the County Council provides a fine bird's-eye view of the parish as it appeared in 1971 (Plate 17). Only about thirty fields now remain. Some of the largest are divided into different cropping areas. As these are liable to vary according to the cropping plan, 'field-names' within the larger whole are, in effect, meaningless.

Only two current field-names refer to acreage. One croft-name has survived as Ashcraft; it was Ashcroft in 1840. The ancient Dennyshwoode has shrunk to a tiny triangular piece of woodland called Dench Wood. In 1840, neighbouring fields called Dench Wood Field, Great and Little Denches and an odd-shaped piece simply called Dench's preserved a vague memory of its original extent.

Apart from these and West Field (discussed above), all the present-day field-names are modern, assigned to suit the new fields. A few, for example White's, Vic Hill's, Fisk's, relate to people who once lived nearby. Most of the others, such as Orchard, Kennels and Barn, relate to features of the area.

Looking back over the long list of place-names gathered together in this survey it seems clear that the manorial names, particularly the topographical ones, have proved the most useful for exploring the past. Research into the landscape became increasingly difficult as the total number of place-names applicable to any specific period declined. This was especially so for the period post-1600 when the use of personal names and acreage names became widespread. However, the personal names to be found in any collection of place-names should not be undervalued. For genealogists and students of social history they are a valuable source of information and indeed it is hoped that this study of the place-names of Woolverstone may offer scope for further research.

Looking to the future, attempting to foresee developments in Woolverstone, as in any rural parish, is peculiarly difficult just now. Great and unprecedented changes in farming practice are imminent. As a conservation area, the village and its immediate surroundings are unlikely to undergo drastic change. Plate 11 shows the area as it is today. Outside this area new forms of land use could alter the landscape considerably. We may see a return to more but smaller fields, new hedges, new woodlands, a wider diversity of crops, more (or less) livestock, even non-agricultural development. But however the landscape evolves there will surely be new place-names to perplex and delight future historians.

APPENDIX
Meanings and derivations

The inexpert linguist searching for place-name meanings must tread very warily, for an 'obvious' explanation is too often wrong. There is only one way to avoid pitfalls and that is to recognise that place-name etymology is a strict discipline with its own established and intricate rules so that, as Dr Margaret Gelling emphasises in her book *Signposts to the Past*, explanations and derivations are a matter for specialists. Dr Gelling's book, which has an extensive bibliography, and *English Place-Name Elements*, edited by A. H. Smith and published for the English Place-Name Society, are essential reference works for local historians studying place-names. Almost all the derivations suggested in this appendix have been found in them. As a first introduction to the subject, an authoritative account is presented in *English Place-Names* by Professor Kenneth Cameron, formerly Honorary Director of the English Place-Name Society. This has, to date, published a large number of place-name surveys, but as yet Suffolk is not among them.

Some of the meanings and derivations proposed in the following list of place-names associated with the manor and parish of Woolverstone (including some belonging to Chelmondiston and Freston) may well provoke argument – even flat contradiction – but if the outcome is a clearer understanding of the history of this small part of Suffolk, then the purpose of this book will have been fulfilled. Further research using sources earlier than those consulted for this study may well provide answers to some of the unsolved puzzles.

In the alphabetical list which follows, the order of presentation is: the name and date; a suggested meaning; the word or words from which the name may be derived, with a references to the sources used. Where appropriate, additional material is offered and discussed. The locality of each place-name is described in chapter III.

The following abbreviations are used: AFr Anglo-French; AN Anglo-Norman; DB Domesday Book; ESax East Saxon; ME Middle English; MedL Medieval Latin; OE Old English; OE(Ang) Anglian; OFr Old French; OFris Old Frisian; ON Old Norse; SOED Shorter Oxford English Dictionary; * a postulated name or element.

AFFOSSWALLE (1590) 'at the ditched embankment' *æt* OE 'at' with *foss* OE 'a ditch' or 'artificially made water channel' (Smith pp 5, 185) and *walla* 'a wall' (Latham). Smith also discussed *foss* as a loan word from Latin *fossa* 'a ditch' or derivation through British, e.g. Welsh *ffos*.

ALCOTS (1495) personal name: Thomas Alcote tenant 1348; William Alcote former holder of tenement ELDEROBORDES 1402.

ALDER CARR see glossary

AMES see EMMES

ARNOLD'S FEN (1491) personal name: Thomas Arnold amerced for poaching 1496; Thomas Arnold in Freston subsidy return.[44] *fenn* OE 'a fen, a marsh, marshland' (Smith, p. 170), locally denoting damp pastureland.

ASHCROFT (1845) ASHCRAFT (current) 'a croft with ash trees' *æsc* OE 'an ash tree' (Smith, p. 4); *croft* see glossary.

BADYLOND (1348) 'land of a man called Badda' OE personal name with *lond* OE, *land* ME 'land' (Smith Pt 2, p. 13). Ralph de Badele witness to a grant of land in Chelmondiston (HD 210/1/7 undated ?13c)

BAKELERS GROVE (1488) personal name: the Bakeler family held manor land in Woolverstone and Chelmondiston for more than two hundred years; Robert juror 1348; Thomas, his son, admitted to two tenements, one messuage and four enclosed fields 1417; John[45] left two grist mills to his son Richard 1481; Thomas bought named places 1544; Thomas Backlar (*sic*) will,[46] 1570, R33/233. *grafa* OE 'a grove' (Smith, p. 208).

BAKELERSLANDS (1492) personal name as above. *lond* OE and *land* ME 'land' or 'a strip of arable land in a common field' (Smith Pt 2, p. 13).

BAKERS FIELD (1628) personal name: no details traced.

BALDWINS (1713) personal name: no details traced. See also BOLDWENNES, BOLDWYNES.

BARK FIELD (1714) 'field associated with the bark of a tree' (i.e. with a tannery) *bark* ME *bork* ON 'bark of a tree'; or possibly a sheepfold *bercaria* MedL and *barkarie* OFr 'a sheepfold' (Smith, p. 20).

BARNECROFT (1523) BERNECROFT (1502) 'a croft by or near a barn' *bere-ærn* OE 'a barn' (Smith, p. 30).

BATAYLLES GROVE (1496) personal name: this wood was held by Margaret daughter of John Bataylle; John Bataylle in subsidy return 1327;[4] in a plea in the manor court 1349; John Bataylle tenant 1460. *Grove* see glossary.

BICKMORES (1787) personal name: John Bickmore occupier of the farm called PUSILLS in Chelmondiston.

BIRCHCROFT (1491) 'a croft with birch trees' *berc* OE 'a birch tree' (Field).

BLITHES (1488) personal name: Christine Blithe, wife of Roger, will[47] 1444.

BOLDWENNES PIGHTLE (1544) BOLDWYNES personal name, but no details traced. *Pightle* see glossary.

BOLDYRODS (1485) personal name: possibly Boldero; Francis Boldero a High Collector of 1568 subsidy.

BORDENMALES (1457) BORDMALES personal name: John de Bordendale in Freston subsidy return[4] of 1327.

BOTTOMS see glossary.

BRADCROFT (1505) 'a croft with a wide or broad piece of land' *brād* OE 'broad, spacious' (Smith, p. 46), or simply 'broad croft'.

BRADSTOK (1402) 'broad tree stump' *brād* OE 'broad' (Smith, p. 460) with *stocc* OE 'a tree trunk, stump or log' (Smith Pt 2, p. 153).

BRAHAM (1410) a manor paying rent to the King (undated rental[48] for Samford Hundred, possibly 14c); Elizabeth Wolverston[5] held a tenement 'of John Braham Kt' 1419; Hugh de Braham's *muselmelne* in Chelmondiston (undated, possibly 14c); Braham Hall, Brantham, home of Thomas Tusser (author of *Five Hundred Points of Good Husbandry*) mid-16c. See also BRAMAPPILION.

BRAKY HEATH (1711) 'a tract of wasteland, overgrown with bracken or fern' *brake* ME 'fern, bracken' (adjective *brakey*) with *hæth* OE(Ang) 'a heath' (Smith, p. 219).

BRAMAPPILION (1508) personal name: John Braham Kt; Richard Pyllion a juryman at Elizabeth Wolverston's IPM[5] 1419. A puzzling combination of two personal names.

BRAMACROFT (1348) possibly the same croft as above but no connection traced.

BRAMPSTONS/BRAMSTONS (1491) personal name: the Bramston (various spellings) family held manor land for many years; Simon and Roger Brandistone in Chelmyngton subsidy return[4] of 1327; Thomas Brandeston held CAKETON and LOPHAMS 1348; Thomas Bramston of Wulferston admitted to land in Wulverston and Chelmondiston called BRAMSTONS 1492; Thomas of Wulferston and Thomas of Chelmundiston both jurors 1495; Thomas Brannston (*sic*) will[49] 1555; Thomas acquired land in Chelmondiston by charter 1590.

BRAMSTONS LANE (1490) 'a lane leading to Bramston's lands' *laning, loning* ME 'a lane, a right of way' (Smith Pt 2, p. 16). This lane was also known as MOWSLOWE LANE at the time; it may well have been the forerunner of the road from Woolverstone to Pin Mill closed by Charles Berners in 1807 after a dispute over rights of way[26] and now a track continuing Richardson's Lane (Chelmondiston) to Pin Mill.

BRAMSTONSLANDS (1524) perhaps 'property of the Bramstons' (Smith, p. 13 'estate' as an alternative to 'strips of land in the common field').

BRATTUCKS (1830) corruption of BROAD OAKS.

BROAD OAKES (1628) 'large oaks' (Smith, p. 45).

le BRODEFELDYS (1413) 'the broad fields' *brād* ME 'broad, spacious' *feld* ME 'unenclosed land held in common for cultivation' (Smith, p. 166). This piece of land in Freston was described as 'two pieces of mollond', i.e. villein land held for money rent (Fisher).

BRODESTOK see BRADSTOK.

BROOME CLOSE (1544) BROOME HILL (1765) 'a close or hill with broom' (*Cytisus scoparius*, a shrubby plant abundant on light land); *clos* OFr *clos(e)* ME 'a close', i.e. 'enclosed piece of land' (Smith, p. 100, adds 'a very frequent element in field-names from 13c, commoner 15c').

BRYCKPHYLD, BRYCKEFFYLDE (1544) 'land where bricks were made'.

BRYGGES (1526) BRIDGES (1620) personal name: Robert Brigge admitted to land formerly BLITHES 1488; Robert Briggs juror 1490 and 1493; Robert Brygys juror 1495; Robert Brygges' will[50] 1504; Robert Heywarde free tenant 1526.

BYLAMS (1702) BYLANDS (1810) possibly 'place or farm near the common fields'. The significance of the element *bi* is discussed by Smith (p. 32); in later OE 'place, house or village' was understood as preceding the element *bi*. Another possibility is that it might be a personal name: a quitclaim to Simon, son of Matthew de Buylin related to lands in Woolverstone and Chelmondiston (SROI HD 210/172, undated, perhaps late 13c).

BYLAM LANE, BYLAM COMMON, BYLAM FARM (all current in Chelmondiston): through place-names, Bylam Farm can be traced back to 1348 common grazing land called PESELYS; BYLAM LANE would have been the way to these common grazings.

CAGES (1689) personal name: no details traced.

CAKETON (1349) The origin of this place is obscure. The element 'ton' (*tūn*) suggests a farmstead, settlement or hamlet (Smith, Pt 1 intro). CAKETON was common grazing land in 1348; William de Caketon listed in 1340 Inquisition[51] under Harkstead; Robert Caketon of Kyrketon (Shotley) in a quit claim[52] over lands in Braham 1410; a tenement called CAKETON 'in the town of Wolverston with its belongings there and in Chelmyngton, Herkested and Holbrook' in Elizabeth Wolverston's IPM[5] 1419.

CAKETONHETH (1460) 'a heath, a tract of uncultivated ground, wasteland overgrown with heather and brushwood' at Caketon: *hæth* OE(Ang) (Smith, p. 219).

CAKETONCROFT (1523) 'a croft at Caketon' or 'Caketon's croft'.

CAKETONYERD (1553) 'an enclosure at Caketon' *geard* OE 'enclosed land by a house, a yard' (Smith, p. 198).

CALVES PIGHTLE (1830) 'a small enclosure for calves'. *Pightle* see glossary.

CALVETON STREET (1612) First element perhaps 'the farm where calves were kept' *calf* OE 'a calf' with *tūn* OE 'farmstead' and *stret* OE(Ang) *stræt* OE *strete* ME 'a paved way or track', possibly of Roman origin (Smith Pt 2, p. 161; Gelling, p. 153, also suggests 'a road of uncertain age with some signs of a made surface'). Current place-names are CALTON COTTAGE and CALTON CREEK, both on the Chelmondiston/Shotley parish boundary.

CHAPPELL FIELD (1567) CHAPPELL LAND (1583) 'land forming the endowment of a chapel' *chapel* (ME).

CHEKERS 'ground of checkered appearance, i.e. mixed soil' (Smith, p. 92, also cites the ME surname Chekker).

CHELENDELONDYS (1521) CHELENDLONDES (1590) The element *Chel-* may be related to *Ceolmund* or to *Ceola* (Smith, p. 89), postulated Saxon settlers; 'the outlying lands of a farm or estate' (Smith, p. 152) *ende* OE 'the end of a place or estate' with *lond* OE, *land* ON 'land' or 'strip of arable land in a common field' (Smith Pt 2, p. 13). These were BRAMSTONSLANDS, *q.v.* As a field name, however, *Chel.* would be an abbreviated form of Chelmondiston, meaning in context 'the border lands of Chelmondiston' rather than directly relating to the OE personal name.

CHELMONDISTON SANTON (1537) 'a farmstead or estate on sandy soil in Chelmondiston' *sand* OE 'sand' (Smith Pt 2, p. 97) with *tūn* OE 'a farmstead'. This was a royal manor in Chelmondiston; Richard Wolverston[53] held lands 'of the Bailiff and Chamberlain of

CHELMONDISTON SANTON'; his forebear Elizabeth Wolverston[5] held 'for her life and in demesne and service of the King in socage as of his soke of Chelmyngton two mills and one hundred and twenty acres of arable and pasture in Chelmyngton and Wolverston'.

CHELMUNDESTON (1174) 'the farmstead or settlement of *Ceolmund*' (Ekwall). The vill of Chelmundeston paid rent of 100 shillings and 10 pence to the King.[48]

CHERDOWNE (1590) The meaning of the element *cher* is obscure; *dūn* OE, *doun* ME 'a hill, an expanse of hill country' (Smith, p. 138).

CHURCH FIELD (1636) Glebe land.

CHYRCHECROFT (1491) 'a croft belonging to the church' *chirche* ME 'church' (Smith, p. 95).

CHYRCHE GATE (1488) 'the way to the church', *gata* ON 'a way, road or path' (SOED).

CHYRCHEWEY (1505) 'the way to the church', possibly from an outlying settlement or hamlet: *weg* OE 'a way, path, road or track – to a place' (Smith Pt 2, p. 249).

CLAPPERS (1505) 'a rabbit warren' *clappere* ME (Field).

CLAY PITS see WATER SHAPE.

le CLEY (1399) the manorial clay pit: *clæg* OE 'clay' (Smith, p. 97). Two fields called CLAPPITS are on the Chelmondiston Tithe Map. See also WATER SHAPE.

THE CLIFF (1628) 'a steep slope or steep bank of a river' *clif* OE *klif* ON (Smith, p. 98).

COLECROFT (1348) 'a croft where charcoal was made' *col* OE 'charcoal' (Smith, p. 105).

COMMONFELD see glossary.

COPTS CORNER (1706) Possibly 'a corner by a copse' *copis* ME 'coppice' (Field).

CORTLEDOWNFFENN (1653) CURTLEDOWNFEN (1672) possibly a personal name OE *Cortel* with either *dun* 'a hill or slope' or *dune* OE adverb 'down below' or 'a place lower than another' (Smith, pp 138-139) and *fenn* OE 'a fen, a marsh' (Smith, p. 170). Topographically this explanation fits the place where the fen lay, between the river Orwell and the west flanks of THE CLIFF. The name became FURTHERDOWN FEN (1744).

CRABBE TREES (1406) 'an orchard of crab apple trees' *crabbe* ME 'a crab apple' (Field) *treow* OE, *tré* ON 'a tree' (Smith Pt 2, p. 110).

CRANES HEATH (1624) personal name: no details traced; heathland owned or occupied by a man called Crane.

CROSSESPIGHTLE (1406) 'a pightle at cross roads' or perhaps a personal name, but no details traced.

CUKKOWYD (1460) 'a wood frequented by cuckoos'; Cuckow, with spelling variations, is a common local surname, but a personal name association is less likely.

CURTELISDONLANDS (1450) perhaps '*Cortel's hill lands'.

CUSSOWOOD (1535) probably the same as CUKKOWYD.

DANECROFT (1528) 'a croft in a valley' *denu* OE, *dænu* ESax 'a valley' (Smith, p. 130).

DEMENSURES HEATH (1624) 'demesne heathland' *demesne* AN, and see glossary.

DENSSHWODE (1348) DENNSSHWOOD (1406) DENNYSSHWODE (1524) 'wood of a man called Denic' personal name OE *Denic* (Mills) with *wudu* OE 'a wood, a tract of woodland' (Smith Pt 2, p. 279).

DONETON (1327) personal name: Nicolas de Doneton in subsidy return[4] of 1327. Possibly 'the farmstead' (*tūn*) of an Anglo-Saxon called Dunna; or 'a hill farm' *dūn* OE 'a hill' (Smith, p. 138, adds that *dūn* is not easily distinguished from *Dunna* in place-names).

DONNEGROVE (1488) 'a grove on a hill'? *dūn* OE, *doun* ME 'a hill or expanse of hill country' (Smith, p. 138).

DONTONSTRETE (1491) 'a Roman track or road in the Dunton area'? *stret* OE(Ang), *stræt* OE and *strete* ME 'a paved way or track' (Smith Pt 2, p. 161; Gelling, p. 153).

DUCK MARSHES (1567) 'haunt of wild fowl'.

DUNTON FENNES (1648) 'damp pasture land in Dunton' *fenn* OE 'a fen, a marsh, marshland' (Smith, p. 170).

DUNTON MEADOWES (1628) 'meadowland in Dunton'.

DUNTON WASTES (1485) 'wasteland or uncultivated land in Dunton'.

DUNTONS PIGHTLE (1749) 'a small piece of enclosed land in Dunton'. See also WALTON: manor records refer to land 'in Dunton' and to 'ditches at Dunton Walton'.

ELBURY DOWN (1683) 'a hill associated with an ancient earthwork, a fortified place or a defended site' *ald* OE 'old' with *burh* OE 'a fortified place' (Smith, p. 58, who adds that if local archaeology and history support alternative derivation, then 'an ancient pre-English earthwork or encampment, an Anglo-Saxon fortification'). A place in

Woolverstone fitting these descriptions is in the Dunton area where Whinney Field Wood now conceals a hill on which there is a level platform of gravelly land, guarded by a deeply cut water-course to the east, a steep slope to the west and a northerly face that descends in two stages, with a flattish area between, to the Orwell shore.

ELDEROBORDES (1406) meaning obscure, perhaps a personal name 'Old Roberts'.

ELVES ACRE (1543) 'the fairies' strip' *elf* OE(Ang) 'a fairy' (Smith, p. 149) and *æcer* OE 'an arable strip in the common field' (Smith, p. 2).

EMMES, EMMS (AMES) personal name: Roger Emme in 1340 Inquisition[51] under Freston.

EMMESCROFT (1544) 'a croft held by the Emmes family'.

EMMESWAY (1490) 'the way to the Emmes' holding' *weg* OE 'a way, path or track – to a place' (Smith Pt 2, p. 249).

EMRYNGALES (1488) 'land held under a bailiff' *ringildus* MedL 'underbailiff or beadle' (Latham). See also CHELMONDISTON SANTON.

ESTFELD (1590) 'one of the manor's Great Fields' (i.e. open arable fields) *feld* ME 'open field, unenclosed land held in common for cultivation' (Smith, p. 166; and see glossary). 'The East Field'.

FALEGATE FELD (1590) 'field at the foldgate' *fald* ME 'fold or sheepfold' (Fisher) and *feld* 'open field' (Smith, p. 166).

FISHBANEWAY (1461) 'the way to Fishbane'. This was the name commonly used for the main road from Ipswich to Shotley. For evidence suggesting a hamlet called FYSHBANE (spelled variously) at or near Shotley see Hervey.[52]

le FLECHERSFELD (1505) 'the land leased or used by a butcher' but more probably a personal name: Thomas Flecher held adjacent land.

FLETCHERS (1492) personal name: Thomas Flecher juror 1460; an occupational name either for a man who fletched arrows or for a butcher: *flesshewer* ME 'a butcher' (Smith, p. 177).

le FOULEWATER (1410) perhaps a decoy pond or expanse of water attracting wild fowl. MERE FIELD, DUCK MARSHES and WATER SHAPE were associated with this area during 16c to 18c; all were lands in Freston close to the Woolverstone parish boundary. A large field called SWAMPY now occupies the area (in both Freston and Woolverstone).

FOUR ACRES, FOWER ACRES (1718) 'a four-acre field'; by this time the word 'acre' had become a measure of area: see glossary.

FOXALL LANE (1505) also FOXHILL, FOXALL HEATH, FOXHOLE, FOXHOLE FIELD, FOXALLS (1718) 'places in an area frequented by foxes' *fox* OE (Field).

FRITH HEATH (1711) 'heath next to woodland' *frith* ME (Smith, p. 190, who adds (p. 219) 'wooded countryside') with *hǣth* OE(Ang) ME 'uncultivated ground'.

le FULLINGMELL (1523) 'a mill for cleansing and thickening woollen cloth' (SOED).

FURTHERDOWN FEN see CORTLEDOWNFEN

FYSHEBANE STRETE (1529) possibly 'a Roman road, track or paved way to or in Fyshebane'; reference[52] to repair in wills of John Strowle 1469 and John Warrey 1529.

FYVE ACRES (1492) 'land five acres in area', five strips of land in a common field, *æcer* OE (Smith, p. 2).

GIBBIS FEN (1505) personal name: no details traced.

GIPESWIC (993) (i.e., Ipswich) 'a place associated with the broad estuary (of the Orwell)' *gip* 'a gap, an opening' (Ekwall); or a personal name: 'the village of Gippa' (Reaney) with *wic* OE denoting 'a dwelling, a farm, a building' (Cameron, pp 147, 151); -*wic* 'Middle-Saxon commercial centre' (Tatton-Brown in Gelling, p. 248).

GODFREYS (1544) personal name: Andrew Godefroy in 1340 Inquisition[51] under Wolfreston. This holding was also referred to as PECKS (*q.v.*).

GODMANCROFT (1491) personal name; Godman held a carucate as a manor in Holbrook in 1086 (DB).

GRACE'S LANE (1684) a misreading of TRACEY'S.

GRENEACRE (1635) possibly related to Church Green in Chelmondiston Tithe Map;[32] *æcer* OE 'an arable strip' (Smith, p. 2).

GRENECROFT (1492) perhaps 'a croft with notably green-coloured land', i.e. marshy (Field), or simply a personal name 'Green's Croft'.

GRETDOWN (1493) 'a gravelly hill' *greot* OE 'gravel' *dūn* OE 'a hill' (Smith pp 209, 138).

GROTESCLOSE (1413) otherwise METHERDONFELD. The significance of *Grotes* is obscure (the word is difficult to read in the court roll). Possibly a personal name, but no details traced; 'a close' *clos* OFr *clos(e)* ME 'an enclosure' (Smith, p. 100, who adds 'a very frequent element in field-names from the 13c, commoner in 15c'). This land was in Freston. The element *Mether* is also obscure, but perhaps a misreading of 'Nether' *neothera, nithera* OE 'lower, under' with *dūn* OE 'a hill' and *feld* ME 'open field' (Smith, pp 138, 166), so perhaps 'the field beside Netherdon, i.e. the lower hill'.

GRYSTMEL (1348) GRYSTMELLES (1481) 'grist mills', mills that ground corn, or malt for brewing, *grist* OE (SOED).

HANDKERCHIEF FIELD (1840 and current) fanciful name for a small field (Field).

HANGING FIELD (1840) 'a field on a steep slope' *hangende* OE 'hanging' (Field).

HARECROFT (1459) 'a croft frequented by hares' *hara* OE 'a hare' (Field) or possibly a personal name: William Harre juror 1521 and 1528.

le HARROW (1544) possibly derived from *hearg* OE 'the site of a pagan shrine or sacred grove'. This name refers to a place in the neighbourhood of Dench Wood. The same place-name occurred in the Chelmondiston Tithe Map[31] referring to a place on high ground east of Pin Mill Lane; in the Freston Tithe Map[54] as a place on a hill at Heathfield Wood (now called Stalls Valley Wood); and in Shotley documented[54] from 1570 to 1834 as lying in Calton (earlier called Calveton) between Kirkton Hall (Shotley Hall) and the Chelmondiston parish boundary. The interpretation of *hearg* is discussed by Gelling, p. 158.

HEGGYNGWODE (1527) 'wood from hedges, used for firewood' *hecg* OE 'a hedge' *wudu* OE 'wood' (SOED)

le HERREYPLETT (1511) perhaps a personal name: William Herre in the subsidy return[44] of 1524; William Harre juror 1528; so 'Herre's plot' *plat* ME 'a small piece of ground' (Field).

THE HILLS (1527) NEWCROFT OR THE HILLS may be Bronze Age burial grounds; for full discussion see chapter VI.

HOBBESCROFT (1508) 'goblins' croft'? *hobbe* OE, *hob* ME 'goblin' (Field); located near ELVES ACRE. Alternatively a personal name: Hob is a diminutive of Robert or Robin.

HOG'S TROUGH (current) probably a corruption of HOBBSCROFT.

HOLCHONCROFT (1531) possibly 'a croft with a corner piece of land' *halk, holke* ME 'corner or nook' (Smith, p. 222).

HOPP GROUND (1714) 'where hops were grown'.

HOWNERS (1636) perhaps a personal name, but no details traced.

HOWTHENCROFT (1491) The element *Howthen* is obscure, possibly a misreading for SOWTHENCROFT 'southern croft'.

HULVERSCROFT (1621) 'a croft with holly trees' *hulvere* ME 'a holly tree' (Smith, p. 268); or, since the site corresponds with WULFELONDCROFT (*q.v.*), a personal name derived from *Wulf* or *Wulfere*.

IPSWICH see GIPESWIC

JIRNETTS or REDS (1403) personal name; no details traced for Jirnetts but see REDS.

JONESCROFT (1485) personal name: John Jones juror 1399.

le KELNE (1497) 'the kiln' *cyln* OE 'kiln, a furnace for baking materials' (Smith, p. 123). Fragments of tiles, some with peg-holes, are abundant on the Orwell shore east of the Freston/Woolverstone parish boundary, where erosion of the river bank has exposed evidence of small kilns packed with tiles. See also TILEHOUSYERD.

KETYLSCROFT (1502) KETTLESCROFT (1686) personal name: nickname derived from *ketill* ON 'cauldron' (Smith Pt 2, p. 3), a round-headed Norseman. *Ketyl* also occurs as an element in various surnames such as Ulfketyl; Kettle is still a common surname locally.

KEWESCROFT possible personal name, but no details traced.

KINE SLADE (1590) 'pasture for cattle in a marshy valley' *kine* archaic plural of 'cow' (SOED) with *slaed* OE(Ang) 'a valley or low, flat marshy ground' (Smith Pt 2, p. 127).

KINNELFELD (1590) meaning obscure.

KLONDYKE (19c) joke name used by workers making a garden in a distant spot behind Woolverstone Hall on the way to Pin Mill[14] (gold had been discovered far away in the Klondyke in 1896).

LAMBARDS otherwise SPETMANS (1544) personal names, but no details traced.

LANE CROFT (1481) 'a croft by a track or lane' *laning* ME 'a lane, a right of way' (Smith Pt 2, p. 13).

LANGLOND (1590) 'a long piece of land' *lang* OE 'long' with *land* OE *lond* ME 'a strip of arable land in a common field' (Smith Pt 2, p. 130).

LANGSTOK (1348) 'a long place' *lang* OE 'long' with *stoc* OE 'a place' (Smith Pt 2, p. 153).

le LEES (1521) 'the pasture or meadowland' *le* OFr 'the' *læs* OE 'pasture or meadowland' (Smith Pt 2, p. 11).

LITIL DOWN (1492) LITLEDOWNE (1520) 'a little hill' *litil* ON 'little' *dun* 'a hill' (Smith Pt 2, pp. 11, 25).

LITILL LOPHAMS (1513) see LOPHAMS

LOCKUM FIELD (1749) probably dative plural of *loca* OE 'an enclosure' (Field) so 'field at the enclosures'.

LONGSTOKHETH (1491) 'a long piece of heathland' *lang* OE 'long' with *stoc* OE 'a place' and *hǣth* OE(Ang) 'a tract of open uncultivated land with brushwood' (Smith, p. 219).

LOPHAMS (1086) personal name: the de Lopham family held the advowson of St Michael's church Woolverstone from 1086 until at least 1349.[41] Roger de Lopham exempted from jury and other services[8] 1319 and listed in the 1327 subsidy return;[4] Lophams and Caketon held by Thomas Brandeston of Chelmyngton 1352; a holding called Lophams listed in the King's rental[48] (possibly 14c); Lophams with the advowson listed with other lands of Elizabeth Wolverston[5] 1419; Henry Gawdy held Lophams 'in Freston and Woolverstone' of Holbrook manor 1579;[56] a messuage called Lophams sold by Philip Catelyn (then lord) 1628, bought by William Berners 1749. LOPHAMS, NORTH and SOUTH, are villages in Norfolk close to the Suffolk border. Ekwall's derivation is *Loppa's Ham* – 'home of Loppa'. A recent history[57] of the Norfolk Lophams makes no mention of a Suffolk connection.

LOPYMFELD (1348) 'an open field belonging to Lophams' *feld* 'open field, unenclosed land held in common for cultivation' (Smith, p. 166).

MABBESDONFELD (1399) personal name: Thomas Mabysyn admitted to a holding in Herkested; with *dūn* OE *doun* ME 'a hill or expanse of hilly country' and *feld* ME 'open field, unenclosed land held in common for cultivation' (Smith, p. 166).

MARCHAMS, MARCHAMTS (1488) personal name, but no details traced; located in Chelmondiston.

le MARSSHE (1523) 'the marsh' *mersc* OE 'a marsh, a watery place' (Smith Pt 2, p. 249).

MARY'S LANE (1628) personal name, but no details traced.

MELWANTWAY, MELWANTWEY (1528) 'the way to the mill' *myln* OE 'mill' with *went* OE 'a path or track' and *weg* OE 'a way, path, road or track – to a place' (Smith Pt 2, p. 249).

MERE FIELD (1567) a field adjacent to WATER CLOSE (*q.v.*); 'field with a pool' *mere* OE.

MERSHMANS (1460) perhaps 'a marshman's holding' *mersc* OE 'a marsh'.

METHERDONFFELD (1413) otherwise GROTESCLOSE. The element *Mether* is obscure; *dūn* OE *doun* ME 'a hill or expanse of hilly land' and *feld* 'open field, unenclosed land held in common for cultivation' (Smith pp 138, 166). Possibly a close taken from, or 'below' a hilly open field; see GROTESCLOSE.

MORESHETH (1460) 'barren heathland' *mōr* OE 'wasteland' (Field) *hæth* OE(Ang) 'uncultivated ground' (Smith, p. 21).

MORMANS PIGHTLE (1413) possibly personal name, but no details traced; or 'Moor man's'.

MOWSLOWE LANE (1490) otherwise BRAMSTONS LANE 'mouse-infested lane by a tumulus' *mūs* OE 'a mouse, a field-mouse' (Smith Pt 2, p. 45) with *hlǣw* OE 'a tumulus' (Mills, p. 16) and *laning* OE 'a lane, a right of way' (Smith Pt, p. 16). A twenty-metre ring ditch is recorded near the lane (present-day Richardson's Lane) as CHEL 014 in the Suffolk County Sites and Monuments files. It is visible only as a crop mark on aerial photograph NMR TM 1937/1/374.

MUSELMELNE (undated, possibly 14c) 'a mouse-infested mill' *mūs* OE 'a mouse, a field-mouse' with *myln* OE 'a mill' (Smith Pt 2 pp 45 and 46). The middle syllable probably represents 'hole'.

MYDDEFEN, MYDDELFFEN (1348) 'the middle part of a damp grazing ground' *middel* OE 'middle' (Field) and *fenn* OE 'a marsh, marshland' (Smith, p. 170). This place was used for common grazing.

NEWBRYGGE (1544) 'Brygge's new holding'. Personal name: see BRYGGES; *niwe* OE 'new, in the sense of newly built' (Smith Pt 2, p. 50).

NEWCROFT OR THE HILLS see THE HILLS

NEWECROFT (1348) 'a new croft' *niwe* 'new, in the sense of newly built' (Smith Pt 2, p. 50).

NEWEHALLE (1488) 'a newly built manor house or hall' *niwe* 'new' (see above) *hall* OE(Ang) 'a hall or large residence' (Smith, p. 225). Probably Chelmondiston Hall, bought by Berners in early 19c, since demolished; site believed to be north of the church on part of present-day Church Farm.

NEWESTRETE (1417) 'a paved way or track possibly of Roman origin' *stret* OE(Ang), *stræt* OE, *strete* ME (Smith Pt 2, p. 161); or 'a road of uncertain age with some signs of a made surface' (Gelling, p. 153).

NEWHOLKE de HANBURGH (HAMMBURGH?) (1489) 'a newly recovered corner piece of ground at *Hanburgh* (i.e., 'high fortified place')' *nīwe* 'new' with *halke* ME 'a corner or nook' (Smith, p. 222) and *hēah* 'high' with *burh*. Less likely is a derivation from *hamm* OE 'an enclosure, meadow or water meadow' (Smith, pp. 229-230) and see also Gelling, p. 43). This description would, however, fit flat land beside the river Orwell in the neighbourhood of ELBURY DOWN (q.v.).

NORTHSTERCHE (1590) 'a northerly stretch of land' *strecche* ME 'a stretch of land' (Smith Pt 2, p. 163).

OLD HOUSE (1723) OLD HOUSE CLIFF (1749) OLD HOUSE LANE (1749) OLD HOUSE FIELD (1749) The Old House was possibly LOPHAMS, *q.v.*; and see also the discussion in chapter VI.

OLDSTRETE LANE (1544) led from Woolverstone to Harkstead.

OLDSTRETEWAY (1491) 'the way to the paved way or track' *stret* OE(Ang) *strēt* OE and *strete* ME 'a paved way or track, possibly of Roman origin' (Smith Pt 2, p. 249) or 'a road of uncertain age with some signs of a made surface' (Gelling, p. 153) and *weg* 'a way, path, road or track – to a place' (Smith Pt 2, p. 249).

OVER THE WAY (1720) in context, a field on the south side of the main Ipswich-Shotley road.

PAILOR FIELD (1718) 'a field enclosed by a fence of pales' *pale* late ME 'a stake used to make a fence' (SOED). Note *pale* also used to denote an area enclosed within a fence, as in 'park pale'. Tailor Field (1830) is a copying error for Pailor.

PAKERSMARSSHE (1423) perhaps 'marshy grazing land' from *pascua* MedL 'feedings, pastures' and *mersc* OE 'a marsh' (Smith Pt 2, p. 39), but the first element is very doubtful. *Paker* may be the occupational surname 'Packer'.

PASCARWODE (1527) perhaps 'a wood pasture' if *pascua* can be taken as above with *wudu* OE 'a wood, a tract of woodland' (Smith Pt 2, p. 3), but the first element is very doubtful.

le PASKER (1423) 'the feedings, pastures': grazing grounds if *pascua* is taken as above.

PEAR TREE CLOSE (1743) 'a close with a pear tree'.

PEAR TREE FIELD (current)

PECKECROFT (1413) personal name: Richard Pyk in Freston subsidy return[4] of 1327.

PECKS or GODFREYS (1544) personal name: Richard Pyk as above and see also GODFREYS. Picks and Pinks (1584) are copying errors for Pecks.

PESELYS (1348) PESEHELLES (1423) PESELL (1459) PESFYLLD (1460) PESYLLYS (1460) le PESELLS (1508) PESSELCLOSE, PESELCLOSE (1528) PESILLS, PUSILLS (1789) personal name: William Pesel[66] conveyed 40 acres of land in Herkested called Grimesdon to Rannulf Bretun, 1206-1207.

PETTS (1734) personal name: John att Pet (1348); John Pett in Freston subsidy return[44] 1524; Henry Pett in Freston subsidy return 1568; Henry Pett's tenement BORDEMALES in Freston included WATERCLOSE (1567).

PEYTENMYNES (1348) meaning uncertain. There may be a reference to peat (*pete* ME) but -*mynes* is unexplainable.

PICKOSTANE (1643) personal name? Richard Pyk, see PECKS; but perhaps a misreading for -lane, thus Pick's or Pyk's Lane.

PICKS, PINKS (1584) copying errors for PECKS.

PICKSOMES, PICKSOMERS (1505) personal name: John Pyksomes amerced for taking five poplar trees from the lord's wood (1348); William Pyckesomyr witness to Robert Bunches' will[51] 1501.

PIN MILL (1781) described as 'a messuage' in a deed of 1781; the name is used generally to describe that part of Chelmondiston that lies beside the river Orwell. There is no mill there now.

PODDS or POYTWYND (1490) personal name; Laurence Pod juror 1410; Laurence and Agnes Pod held land in Wulferston and Freston 1413 (PODDS). Perhaps POYT became POYNT (*q.v.*); *wynd* OE ME 'a narrow passage or turning off a main thoroughfare' (SOED) *wind* OE 'something winding, a winding path' (Smith Pt 2, p. 268).

POMPARDS (1485) possibly personal name, but no details traced.

POTTS PIGHTLE (1718) probably personal name, perhaps misreading of PODD.

POY FIELD (1544) and le HARROW: the meaning of POY is obscure, but the word appears to have been abbreviated by the scribe using a straight line above the word: if 'n' were meant, then PONY FIELD could be the meaning, except that *pony* is very rare in field names.

le POYNT (1505) obscure.

PRESTYLBROOK (1497) 'brook next to the tileyard meadow' *pre* OFr and ME 'a meadow' (Smith Pt 2, p. 72). This brook is the Freston/

Woolverstone parish boundary, adjacent to the TILEHOUSYERD (*q.v.*).

PRINNYS (1505) personal name, but no details traced.

le PURLIEU (1711) 'place at the edge of a wood' *purley* ME (Field).

PURPETTE (1495) William Tendryng amerced for default, owing suit of court for this holding.

PURPETYD (1497) William Tenderyng still in default.

PURTEPET (1348, 1406) personal name: Walter Purtepet grazed a cow and a mare in the lord's pasture; William Purtepet grazed two foals, sheep and lambs in the lord's pasture.

PURTEPYT (1086) an unidentified Domesday manor of sixty acres in the Samford Hundred.[58] Osbern, a freeman, held this manor of Richard son of Earl Gilbert both before and after the Conquest. The significance of the element *purte* is obscure. P. H. Reaney[59] suggested that it might be connected with water, citing Purfleet (*Pyrteflyte* 1285) in Essex; Portpool (*Purtepol* 1203) in Middlesex; a spring or stream in Manuden, Essex, called *Purtewelle*; and a lost *Potchmeers* having a 13c form *Purtemere*, also in Essex. E. Martin[60] recently reported *Purtepol* (1251) in Hitcham, Suffolk, which appears to be identical in name with *Purtepol* (1203) in Essex. The element *pytt* OE(Ang) 'a pit, a natural hollow' (Smith Pt 2, p. 75) with *purte* suggests 'a pit or hollow connected in some way with water'. The association of PURTEPYT with the manor of Wolverston Hall places it on the Shotley Peninsula. William Tendryng (see also PURPETTE, PURPETYD above) held land of the manor until *c.*1500. Purtepyt appears to have extended across three parish boundaries: Woolverstone, Harkstead and Chelmondiston. William de Pourtepet was tax assessor for Herkested for the 1327 subsidy;[61] William Tenderyng, lord of the manor of Herkested cum Clymston from 1474[62] until 1499, willed 'that his lands called Purpettes in Herkested be sold';[63] Thomas Abell was amerced for removing a hedge on the Processional Weye, Herkested, 1582.[64] A spring rises in a field in Chelmondiston called Spring Cover, adjacent to parts of fields called Clappits and Gravel Pit Fields (Tithe Map, Chelmondiston),[32] the greater part of these fields being in Harkstead. This conjunction of water and pits supports the derivation of Purtepyt suggested above and also places on the map the hitherto unidentified Domesday manor of Purtepyt.

PYN MILL (1781) 'a mill with a penned water supply' *pynd* OE 'an enclosure, a pool, or pond' (Smith Pt 2, p. 25). It was the manorial fulling mill. Banks that penned the water are faintly discernible in the valley overlooked from Pin Mill car park.

PYNMYLL (1498) also described as 'the lord's house or close' from which John Welles of Ipswich stole twelve barrels of beer.

QUINNS (1830) possibly personal name, but no details traced; or possibly 'an old woman's holding' *cwene* OE 'a woman' (Field).

RAINBOW (1718) 'land with a curved boundary', so ploughed in curves (Reaney, p. 600). The only markedly curved boundary in Woolverstone is Harkstead Lane, so this field (now Handkerchief Field) was probably adjacent to it.

REDS (1493) personal name: Simon de Rede in 1340 Inquisition;[51] Walter and Willian Reed jurors 1348; Roger Reed juror 1399.

ROBYNS CLOSE (1410) personal name, but no details traced.

ROCKETTS GROVE (1410) perhaps 'a rookery' *hrōc* OE 'a rook' (Field).

RUNTYNGS (1327) RUNTINGS (1742) personal name: Simon Runtyng in 1327 subsidy return;[4] Thomas Runtyng rector of Woolverstone 1399; a holding 'formerly Runtings' granted to William Bramston 1488.

SANDPETTES (1348) '[manorial] sandpits' *pytt* OE 'a pit' (Smith Pt 2, p. 75).

SANFORD (GREAT, SMALL) (1714) 'fields by a sandy ford'? *sand* OE 'sand' with OE *ford* (Field).

SARJENTS, SARGEANTS HEATH (1621) personal name: John Sargent amerced for failing to mend his fence 1528.

SEBBYNGSCROFT (1309) personal name, but no details traced.

SHAMBLES (GREAT, LITTLE) (1619) 'a stall for displaying meat for sale' *sceamol, scamol* OE 'a shambles' (Smith Pt 2, p. 100). They were simply fields in 1619 but earlier had perhaps been connected with a meat market. They occupied land adjacent to the main road and to Foxall (Glebe) Lane, an easily accessible crossroads. See also FLETCHERS.

SHAMBLES CLOSE (1636) 'a close where meat was – or had been – sold'.

SHAMELE (1491) 'a shelf of land'? (Smith Pt 2, p. 100) or *scamella* ME 'market stall' (Latham). This was not the same place as the two SHAMBLES fields.

SHARPELLS (1826) probably a personal name, but no details traced.

SHELENCLYFFE, CHELENDCLYFFE (1497) 'a steep slope or cliff in Chelmondiston' (see also CHELENDELONDYS) *clyf* OE, *klif* ON 'a steep slope or steep river bank' (Smith, p. 98). The Chelmondiston Tithe Map[32] shows Cliff Meadow adjacent to saltings between Pin

Mill and the Woolverstone parish boundary. There is also a much higher cliff east of Pin Mill, known today as The Cliff.

SHOLANDE (1327) personal name: Matilda de Sholande in 1327 subsidy return[4] for Chelmyngton and Wolferston. The surname Sholande derived from OE *scohland* MedL *solanda* 'shoeland, land bequeathed for the provision of footwear for a monastery' (Hart, EP-NS J,4,1972).

SHRUBBS (1670) 'a place covered with underwood, broom or brushwood' *scrybb* OE 'shrub' (Reaney, p. 377).

le SLADE (1492) 'a valley or low flat marshy ground' *slæd* OE(Ang) (Smith Pt 2, p. 127).

SMART FIELD (1714) possibly 'rich pasture land' *smeoru* OE 'fat, grease or lard' usually an allusion to rich butter-making pasture (Smith Pt 2, p. 130), though modern 'smart' seems just as likely.

SOWTHEFELD (1544) 'South Field' in Freston, a former Great (open) Field.

SPETMANS (1544), alternative name for LAMBARDS, LAMBERTS (personal names, but no details traced); Thomas Spetman held in a tenement in Freston and Woolverstone, died 1523; Thomas Spetman juror 1535.

SPRINGSWELLECROFT (1535) 'a croft with a spring in a young plantation' *spring* ME 'a young shoot, young plantation, a copse' (Smith Pt 2, p. 140) with *wella* OE 'a spring' (Field).

STREPENCROFT (1481) unexplained.

STUTTONS (1495) personal name, but no details traced.

SWAMP (1804) SWAMPY (current) 'a boggy place' (see also WATERSHEEPES and WATERCLOSE).

SYNTHONS (1489) meaning obscure.

SYRIGROVE meaning obscure.

TAILOR FIELD (1830) a copying error for PAILOR.

le THORNS (1491) le THORNE (1531) 'the area invaded by thorns': possibly the same place as SYNTHONS.

THREACRES (1399) 'a holding formed from three arable strips in the common field' *æcer* OE 'an arable strip' (Smith Pt 2).

TRACEY'S LANE (1753) led to Tracey's Field: *laning, loning* ME 'a lane, a right of way' (Smith Pt 2, p. 16).

TRACEY'S LANE FIELD (1719) personal name: Robert Tracey, former owner.

TRUEFORDS (1711) possibly a personal name, but no details traced.

TYLERS (1734) personal name, but no details traced.

TYLHOUSYERD, OLD and NEW (1497) 'enclosure where tiles were made' *tigel* OE 'a tile' with *geard* 'a yard' (Smith Pt 2 pp. 179, 198).

TYLKYLNYERD (1548) 'enclosure containing a kiln' *cyln* OE 'a kiln' (Smith, p. 123).

UNDERWOODE (1544) 'a piece of coppiced woodland'.

le VANT (1495) 'the water channel' *vente* ME 'an outlet' (Field).

WALSHER (1348) meaning obscure.

WALTON (1491) possibly 'farmstead of the Britons' OE *Weala* 'of the Britons' with *tūn* OE 'farmstead' (Smith Pt 2, p. 244 and Pt 1 intro). Alternatively 'a walled farm' or 'a farmstead protected by a surrounding rampart', *wall, weall* OE 'a wall' with *tūn* as above. Without earlier forms of the name it is impossible to decide which of the meanings suggested is the more likely. The area is believed to be adjacent to ELBURY DOWN. The name also occurs in DONTON WALTON. It may be significant that WALTON FERRY, WALTON LOWER STREET and WALTON lie a few miles away in Felixstowe, where there was a Roman shore fort, now lost beneath the sea. This WALTON was *Waletuna* (DB) 'a farmstead or village of the Britons' (Mills, p. 344).

WARBYLTONS (1523) personal name: Thomas Warbilton juror 1490-1498; a 'former tenant' 1502; possibly John Warburton, tenant 1459.

WARDECROFT (1348), WARDESCLOSE (1459) personal name, but no details traced.

WATER CLOSE (1567) 'an enclosure next to water'.

WATERSHEEP, WATERSHEPE (1410) 'a conduit, a water channel, an expanse of water' *waeterscipe* OE (Smith Pt 2, p. 238). Since this place was associated with le FOULEWATER (*q.v.*), an expanse of water seems the most appropriate interpretation.

WATERSHEEPES or WILLISLANDE (1610); WATERSHAPE or WILLY'S LAND (1707) later versions of the same place-name (WATERSHEEP), when presumably the open water had become overgrown with willows: *willig* OE 'a willow' (Smith Pt 2, p. 266). This land was in Freston, almost certainly now part of Swampy, but formerly associated with MERE FIELD, WATER CLOSE and DUCK MARSHES (le FOULEWATER?), *q.v.*

WATYRYATTE (1523) 'a sluice gate'. The court roll adds in explanation 'Porta Aquatica'.

WELL MEADOW (1628) 'meadow with a spring in it' *wella* OE 'a spring' (Smith Pt 2, p. 250).

le WEND (1497) 'the path' *wante* ME 'a path' (Smith Pt 2, p. 245).

WERRYES (1497) personal name: George Warrye juror 1528 and 1554.

WEST CROFT (1460) possibly 'a croft in West Field'.

WESTEFELDE (1460) WESTFILD (1485) 'one of the manor's Great Fields' *feld* ME 'an open field, unenclosed land held in common for cultivation' (Smith, p. 166).

WEST FIELD (1714 and current) 'part of the former Westefelde'.

WHARTELANDS (1826) possibly the same place as WHERTELANDS.

WHEAT MEADOW (1714) 'meadow formerly a wheat field'.

WHERTELANDS (1544) 'an area where vegetables or herbs were grown' *wyrt OE* 'a herb' (Smith Pt 2, p. 282). Alternatively: 'strips lying across others' from *þverr* ON 'athwart'. These were George Warry's lands (see WERRYES).

WHETCROFT (1461) 'a croft where wheat was grown' *hwǣte* OE 'wheat' (Smith Pt 2, p. 271).

WHINNEY FIELD (1628 and current) 'a field with whin (gorse or furze)' *hvin* ON 'whin' (Smith Pt 2, p. 270). Now a clean arable field.

WHITE HOUSE FARM (current) a farmhouse built of white bricks, lying next to the Woolverstone/Harkstead parish boundary.

WHITING STREET (1707) 'a way' *strǣt* OE and *strete* ME 'a track', possibly associated with John Whytyng's holding (see below) and possibly of Roman origin (Smith Pt 2, p. 161 and Gelling, p. 153); see also chapter V.

WHYTYNGS (1488) WHITINGE (1670) personal name: John Whytyng tenant 1460 of a holding 'in Holbrook and in Harksted', so presumably it lay across the parish boundary.

WOLF MEADOW (1744) and CORN MEADOW appear to have been the same place.

WOLFRESTONS PIGHTLE (1624) personal name: the Wolfreston family name, spelled variously Wolferston, Wulferston, Wolverston.

WOOLVERSTONE (current) a small Suffolk parish: the final 'e' was added to the name in the late 18c, probably by the Berners family, but was not in common use until the early 20c. Earlier spellings include ULFERESTUNA, HULFERESTUNA (DB 1086) WOLFERSTON (FF 1196).

MEANINGS OF WOOLVERSTONE'S PLACE-NAMES

WOOLVERSTONE FIELD (1714) a field in Chelmondiston adjacent to the Woolverstone parish boundary.

WOOLVERSTONE PARK approximately 300 acres of ornamental parkland, the former seat of the Berners family.

WRAYNECROFT (1636) perhaps 'a croft with a crooked piece of land' from *vrangr* ON 'crooked' (Field), but this seems doubtful.

WRENSPARKE (1839) usually a joke name of a very small piece of ground, in this instance a very small wood. On the Harkstead Tithe Map it is WRENS PARK (1839) and currently RENCE PARK.

WULFELONDCROFT (1502) 'a croft associated with Wulf's lands' *lond* ME 'land, a strip of land in an open field' (Smith Pt 2, p. 13). This was a substantial holding including a messuage and nine buildings, possibly that land named HULVERSCROFT in 17c land transactions.

GLOSSARY

acre
A strip of arable land, an individual holding in a common field; later, simply a piece of arable land; now a unit of area.

advowson
The right to present a clergyman to a benefice (living).

aerial photographs
These can reveal the hidden presence of any former feature that once disturbed the soil. Uneven crop growth causes shadows which are distinctly apparent, especially in cereal crops on light land during drought conditions. Photographed obliquely from the air early or late in the day these shadows or marks indicate where the surface conceals old foundations, ditches, boundaries or former tracks. The camera may record a single feature or a series relating to different periods.

alder carr
A wood of alder (*Alnus glutinosa*); they flourish in a moist, marshy habitat.

amercement
The common term denoting a fine imposed in a manorial court for a misdemeanour. The offender was 'in the lord's mercy' and liable to a penalty (fine).

archaeological fieldwork
Exploration that does not entail excavation. *See* field walking; metal detecting.

archaeological periods
Bronze Age: 2000 to 700 BC; Iron Age: 700 BC to 43 AD; Roman: 43 to 410; Early Saxon: 410 to 650; Middle Saxon: 650 to 850; Late Saxon/Norman: 850 to 1150; Medieval: 1150 to 1450; Post-medieval: 1450 onwards.

bottoms
Low-lying land, land at the lowest point.

braky, breaky
Heathland with bracken or brushwood.

campus
Medieval Latin term for an unenclosed or open field.

carucate
A measure of land used in the Domesday Survey: the amount of land that could be ploughed in a year with one plough and sufficient to feed a family. It varied, according to soil type and terrain, from 60 to 180 modern acres.

causeway
A raised road or path.

close
A small enclosure, originally from an open field.

commonfeld	Open or unenclosed land on which manorial tenants held grazing rights.
copyhold	A form of manorial tenure by which property was held of a manor by copy of court roll.
cover	A thicket hiding game.
croft	A small enclosure usually with a house adjacent.
crop marks	*See* aerial photographs.
demesne	Manor land retained by the lord for his own use, the manor farm.
demise	To convey or transfer an estate by will or lease.
drift	A track leading to fields along which livestock were driven.
enfeoff	To put a tenant legally in possession of a holding, or to surrender a holding.
Escheator	An official appointed by the Crown to collect any revenues due when an estate reverted to the Crown or to the lord. The office was introduced in 1195.
feld, fyld, field, Field	Originally open country; then enclosed land used for agriculture, a main division of the common arable land (a Great Field such as Westefeld); from the 14c onwards field came to mean a smaller enclosed unit – although modern fields are now often 'great'.
fen, fenn	Damp pasture or marshy land.
field walking	Systematic exploration of a specific area to locate pottery sherds, worked flints and other potentially interesting objects lying on the surface of arable land. Undertaken only with the landowner's permission and always involving the meticulous recording of each find and its location on a site report sheet for expert scrutiny.
fine	Payment required by the manor court on a change of tenancy of manor lands; also imposed for a variety of misdemeanours.
frith	Land at the edge of a wood.
glebe	Land forming part of a clergyman's income.
Glebe Terrier	An inventory of glebe land.
Great Fields	Open fields.
grove	A small wood or group of trees.

grovetta	A smaller wood.
holding	A tenement 'held of the manor'; they usually bore the name of the tenant.
IPM	Inquisition post mortem: an enquiry held by an Escheator aided by a local jury following the death of a tenant-in-chief of the King, to establish the date of death, the age of the heir and the lands held. The system was introduced in the reign of Henry III.
land, lond	Arable land; a strip in a common field; a 'piece of land'.
lane	A track, byway or road between hedges.
language periods	Old English: used from the beginning of the English settlement until about 1150; Middle English: from *c.*1150 to *c.*1500; Modern English: from 1500 onwards.
lees, leys	Meadow or pasture.
manor	Originally a feudal, territorial and economic unit introduced into England by the Normans after 1066 (OF *manoir*). The lord of the manor was either a tenant-in-chief directly of the King, or a tenant of an overlord. The people who lived in the manor 'held of the lord'. The systems were based on clearly defined customs, rights and obligations. Customary tenants of the manor held land in return for labour services; freehold tenants paid rent; and copyholders held at the will of the lord, with their service obligations commuted to rent and their title written into the manor court roll.
manor court	The lord of the manor was empowered to hold Courts Baron and Courts Leet. The former governed the use of common fields, wastes and tenancies; the latter dealt with petty offences. By the fourteenth century in Woolverstone, General Courts combined these functions. Attendance at the courts – suit of court – was obligatory. Those absent without valid reason were fined. The jury comprised freehold and copyhold tenants. Court proceedings were recorded in medieval Latin (usually abbreviated) until English was adopted during the eighteenth century.
meadow	Land for mowing.

GLOSSARY

messuage
In theory, a house erected before the time of legal memory, that is, the reign of Richard I, but the term was commonly used to describe houses built before living memory. It sometimes covered outbuildings, yards, garden and orchard. A 'capital messuage' was a large house.

metal detecting
A technique used in archaeological fieldwork to detect the presence of metal objects such as coins below the soil surface, exploring systematically and recording and reporting as in field walking. The landowner's permission is essential.

office
A field near a building associated with a small-scale agricultural or industrial enterprise; for example, malting.

pannage
Payment by manorial tenants for the right to pasture their pigs in the lord's woods.

pasture
Grassland for grazing.

piece
Originally part of a larger field; later simply synonymous with field; often identified by combining with a personal name.

pightle
A small enclosure.

plough-team
Eight oxen; some teams belonged to the lord and were worked on his behalf, others were owned by the men.

purlieu
Land at the edge of a wood.

quit claim
A formal discharge or renunciation of a claim, by the sellers of land or property.

rainbow
Refers to land ploughed concentrically or with a curved boundary.

soc (Soke)
A right of local jurisdiction.

South Sea Bubble
A speculation mania that ruined many English investors in 1720. It centred on the South Sea Company, founded in 1711 to trade, mainly in slaves, with Spanish America. After a boom in the early months of 1720, which caused the share price to rise dramatically, a sudden steep fall towards the end of the year led to ruin for the speculators.

strips   Sub-divisions of furlongs (furrow lengths) in the manor Great Fields. Each was held by individual tenants and identified by his name. When the strips were enclosed the resulting close or croft took the tenant's name. In time, as the tenancies changed so did the place-names. Enclosure was so far advanced in Woolverstone in the fourteenth century that only one reference to strips appears in the manor court roll.

suit of court   Attendance at court; *see* manor court, above.

REFERENCES

1   Ekwall, E., *The Concise Oxford Dictionary of English Place-names*, 4th edn (Oxford, 1966).

2   *ibid.*

3   Scarfe, N., *Suffolk in the Middle Ages* (Woodbridge, 1986), p. 26.

4   Hervey, S. H. A. (ed.), *Suffolk in 1327, being a Subsidy Return*, Suffolk Green Books No. ix (Woodbridge, 1906), p. 2.

5   *IPM* 1419 Elizabeth Wolferston, PRO C.138/40/1, translated in Hervey, S. H. A. (ed.), *Shotley Parish Records*, Suffolk Green Books, No. xvi vol. 2 (Bury St Edmunds, 1912), pp. 19-21.

6   Woolverstone Hall Manor Court Roll, 1348-1640. SROI S1/10/5.1 fols 1, 2 1348/49/52.

7   *Burke's Landed Gentry*, 18th edn (London, 1972), vol. 3 (under Pipe-Wolferstan of Statford).

8   Pat. Rolls, Cal. Richard II, in Copinger, W. A. (ed.), *Suffolk Records and Manuscripts*, vol. 5 (London, 1904), p. 436.

9   SROI S1/10/4.9.

10 Woolverstone Hall Manor Court Book: Steward's File 1711-1791. SROI S1/10/5.5.

11 Briggs, N., 'Woolverstone Hall: Some Reflections on the Domestic Architecture by John Johnson (1732-1814)', *Proc. Suffolk Inst. Archaeol.*, xxxiv (1977), pp. 59-64.

12 Handwritten extract from Richardson, A. E., *Robert Mylne, Architect and Engineer 1733-1811* (London, 1955), refers to Mylne's visit to Woolverstone Park, September 1791, to discuss obelisk. H. Wilton's Collection of Historical Notes and Cuttings: SROI HD 672/1/65.

13 Jones, B., *Follies and Grottoes*, 2nd edn (London, 1974), p. 393.

14 Todd, R. J. U., *c.*1930. Unpublished lecture and notes on Woolverstone. SROI qs Woolverstone 9.

15 Department of the Environment. List of Buildings of Special Architectural and Historic Interest. Babergh District Council, List No. 35, 29 July 1987 SROI.

16 Henry Davy, engraving of Woolverstone Church, May 22, 1838, in SROI Fitch Collection HD 480/1.

17 Acts of the Norwich Consistory Court: drawings, specifications and correspondence. NRO CON 153/1888/89.

18 Will 1492, Robert Wolverston, PRO PROB 11/10.

19   Lutyens, E., Drawings for St Peter's House, Woolverstone (1901) [British Architectural Library, London]; Whitehouse, J., *Woolverstone House, Suffolk* (forthcoming).

20   Babergh District Council, Suffolk, Plan of Woolverstone Conservation Area, designation date 15 November 1989.

21   Tooley, P., *Operation Quicksilver* (Romford, 1988), and 'The Sailor's Tale', chapter 9 in *Trojan Horse: Deception Operations in the Second World War*, by Martin Young and Robbie Stamp (Mandarin Books, 1991), pp. 108-13.

22   'Nautical Training School', *East Anglian Daily Times* (28 January 1947).

23   'LCC Boarding School', *Municipal Journal* (7 January 1951).

24   Woolverstone Hall Planning Brief, Babergh District Council, March 1990.

25   Woolverstone Tithe Map 1840. SROI FDA 2998/A1/1b (map) and FDA 298/A1/1a (apportionment).

26   Roads to Chelmondiston from Woolverstone, with plan, 1807. SROI S1/10/10 and S1/10/10.3.

27   Newman, J., 'East Anglian Kingdom Survey – Final Interim Report on the South East Suffolk Pilot Field Survey', *Bulletin of the Sutton Hoo Research Committee*, No. 6 (1989), pp. 17-20.

28   WLV 008. County Sites and Monuments Records (CSMR), Archaeology Section, Suffolk County Council Planning Department, Shire Hall, Bury St Edmunds.

29   (a) Cambridge Collection of Air Photographs: BXI-34; and (b) Royal Commission for Historical Monuments (England) NMR TM 1838/1/216 in CSMR.

30   Royal Commission for Historic Monuments (England) NMR TM 1937/1/374 in CSMR.

31   Suffolk Archaeological Unit AGM 25 and 26, 4 August 1977, in CSMR.

32   Chelmondiston Tithe Map 1839. SROI FDA 62/A1/1b (map) and FDA 62/A1/1a (apportionment).

33   WLV 015, CSMR.

34   RCHM(E) Neg. No. 826, Frame No. 218, 7 July 1975; NMR TM 1838/1/218 in CSMR.

35   Hodskinson, J., *The County of Suffolk Surveyed* [1783], ed. with an Introduction by D. P. Dymond, Suffolk Records Society, vol. xv (1972).

36   Schedule of the Berners' Woolverstone Estate Lands, 1830. SROI S1/10/4.1.

37   Pencil sketch of the 'old' Woolverstone Hall, late 18c. Fitch Collection. SROI HD 480/1.

38   Exchange of Glebe land, Woolverstone Rectory, with plan 1817. SROI FF2/32/1.

39   SROI S1/10/5.11.

40   SROI S1/10/3.1.

REFERENCES

41   Tanner, Index of Institution Books, vol. ii, Samford Deanery. NRO.

42   Klaiber, A. J., *The Story of the Suffolk Baptists* (London, 1931).

43   An accurate survey of an estate belonging to Mr John Leggatt, draper, of Ipswich, lying in Woolverstone, Suffolk. Plan (undated, late 18c/early 19c) with field names. SROI S1/10/11.29 and HE7 BL 2855 Gp 1/3.

44   Hervey, S. H. A. (ed.), *Suffolk in 1524, being the Return for a Subsidy in 1523, with a Map of Suffolk in Hundreds*, Suffolk Green Books No. x (Woodbridge, 1910), p. 306.

45   Will 1481, John Bakeler. SROI IC/AA2/3/1.

46   Will (Chelmondiston) 1570, Thomas Backlar. SROI R23/233.

47   Will 1444, Christine Blithe. SROI J421/1.

48   Rental of the Lord King for Samford. SROI S1/13/25.1, undated possibly 14c.

49   Will 1556, Thomas Brannston (*sic*). SROI J421/3.

50   Will, 1504, Robert Brygges. SROI IC/AA1/3/1.

51   Partridge, Charles S., 'Suffolk Surnames in 1340, from Non. Inqu. Curia Scaccari Temp. Reg. Ed. III', in *East Anglian Notes and Queries*, New Series, vol. v (1893-4), p. 259.

52   Hervey, S. H. A. (ed.), *Shotley Parish Records*, Suffolk Green Books No. xvi, vol. 2 (Bury St Edmunds, 1912), p. 122.

53   *IPM* 1537, Richard Wolverston. PRO C 142/61/33.

54   Freston Tithe Map 1841. SROI FDA 107/A1/1b (map) and FDA 107/A1/1a (apportionment).

55   Hervey, *Shotley Parish Records*, vol. 2, p. 477.

56   Holbrook Manor Court Book 1579. SRO S1/10/9.

57   Serpell, M. F., *A History of the Lophams* (Chichester, 1980).

58   Rumble, A. (ed.), *Domesday Book 34: Suffolk*, 2 vols (Chichester, 1986), entry 25.66.

59   Reaney, P. H. (ed.), *The Place-names of Essex*, English Place-Name Society, vol. xii (Cambridge, 1935).

60   Martin, E., in *Proc. Suffolk Inst. Archaeol.*, xxxvii (1991), p. 193.

61   Hervey, S. H. A., *Suffolk in 1327*, No. ix, p. 3.

62   Manor of Herkested cum Clymston, Court Rolls, Society of Genealogists' abstract and translation; Court 13 Ed. IV SROI 52/6/14.7.

63.   Will of William Tendering, 1501. PRO PROB 11/12.

64   Manor of Herkested cum Clymston, Court Roll 24 Eliz.

65   Hervey, *Shotley Parish Records*, vol. 2, p. 131.

66.   Dodwell, B. (ed.), *Feet of Fines for the County of Suffolk in the Reign of King John 1194-1214* (London, Pipe Roll Society, 1956), entry 470, p. 225.

BIBLIOGRAPHY

1. Documentary Sources
Suffolk Record Office Ipswich (SROI)
    Redstone Index:
        S1/10 series Berners Estate
        S1/10/5.1 5.5 Manorial
    Bidwell's Documents
        HE7 2855 & 2806
        HD 169/2 estate accounts
        HB9 S1/11/1-5 Manor
    Parish Records
        FB 199
    Glebe Terriers
        W114 564/W 1706 1912
    Probate Records
        Calendar of Wills, Archdeaconry of Suffolk, vols I & II 1444 1700
Norfolk Record Office (NRO)
    Diocesan Records
Public Record Office (PRO)
        Inquisitions post mortem
        PCC Wills

2. Published Sources

Aston, M. and Rowley, T., *Landscape Archaeology* (Newton Abbot: David and Charles, 1974)

Bennett, H. S., *Life on an English Manor: a Study of Peasant Conditions 1150-1400* (Gloucester: Alan Sutton, 1987)

Cameron, Kenneth, *English Place-Names*, 4th edn (London: Batsford, 1988)

Darby, H. C. (ed.), *A New Historical Geography of England* (Cambridge: Cambridge University Press, 1976)

Dodgston, R. A. and Butler, R. A. (eds), *An Historical Geography of England* (London: Academic Press, 1978)

Douglas, D. C., *The Social Structure of East Anglia*, Oxford Studies in Social and Legal History, 9 (Oxford: Clarendon Press, 1927)

Dymond, D., *Archaeology and History* (London: Thames and Hudson, 1974)

Dymond, D. and Northeast, P., *A History of Suffolk* (Chichester: Phillimore, 1985)

Dymond, D. and Martin, E. (eds), *An Historical Atlas of Suffolk*, 2nd edn (Ipswich: Suffolk County Council and Suffolk Institute of Archaeology and History, 1989)

BIBLIOGRAPHY

Elton, G. R. (ed.), *England 1200-1640. The Sources of History: Studies in the Uses of Historical Evidence* (Ithaca, New York and London: Camelot Press, 1969)

Field, J., *English Field-Names: A Dictionary* (Newton Abbot: David and Charles, 1972)

Fisher, J. L. and Powell, W. R. (eds), *A Medieval Farming Glossary of Latin and English Words (Taken Mainly from Essex Records)* (London: National Council of Social Service for the Standing Conference for Local History, 1968)

Gelling, M., *Sign-posts to the Past: Place-Names and the History of England*, 2nd edn (Chichester: Phillimore, 1987)

Hone, N., *The Manor and Manorial Records*, 2nd edn (London: Methuen, 1912)

Hoskins, W. G., *The Making of the English Landscape*, 2nd edn (London: Hodder & Stoughton, 1977)

Hoskins, W. G., *Fieldwork in Local History*, 2nd edn (London: Faber & Faber, 1982)

King, E., *England 1175-1425* (London: Routledge & Kegan Paul, 1979)

Mills, A. D., *A Dictionary of English Place-Names* (Oxford: Oxford University Press, 1991)

Platt, C., *Medieval England: a Social History and Archaeology from the Conquest to AD 1600* (London: Routledge, 1978)

Powell, E., *The Rising in East Anglia in 1381, with an Appendix Containing the Suffolk Poll Tax Lists for that Year* (Cambridge: Cambridge University Press, 1896)

Rackham, O., *The History of the Countryside* (London: Dent, 1986)

Reaney, P. H., *The Origin of English Place-Names* (London: Routledge Kegan Paul, 1960)

Riley, D. N., *Air Photography and Archaeology* (London: Duckworth, 1987)

Rogers, A. and Rowley, T. (eds), *Landscapes and Documents* (London: National Council of Social Service for the Standing Conference for Local History, 1974)

Rowley, T. (ed.), *Saxon Settlement and Landscape. Papers presented to a Symposium Oxford 1973*, British Archaeological Reports, British Series (Oxford: BAR, 1974)

Rumble, A. (ed.), *Domesday Book 34: Suffolk*, 2 vols (Chichester: Phillimore, 1986)

Scarfe, N., *The Suffolk Landscape*, 2nd edn (Bury St Edmunds: Alastair Press, 1987)

Smith, A. H. (ed.), *English Place-Name Elements, Parts I and II*, English Place-Name Society, vols xxv and xxvi (Cambridge: Cambridge University Press for the EPNS, 1956)

Taylor, C., *Village and Farmstead: A History of Rural Settlement in England* (London: George Philip, 1964)

Taylor, C., *Fields in the English Landscape* (London: Dent, 1975)

Taylor, C., *Roads and Tracks in Britain* (London: Dent, 1979)

Taylor, C. and Muir, R., *Visions of the Past* (London: Dent, 1983)

Wilson, D. M. (ed.), *The Archaeology of Anglo-Saxon England* (Cambridge: Cambridge University Press, 1976)

Wilson, D. R., *Air Photographic Interpretation for Archaeologists* (London: Batsford, 1982)

INDEX OF PERSONAL NAMES

The following index to personal names in the book was compiled by the publisher, Shaun Tyas. Variant spellings of names are preserved. Occasions of surnames without identifying first names are treated as references to the family. Christian names without surnames are also included. Multiple references to the same name on one page are given only one reference. Some of the names included here are personal names identified as occuring within names of places, such as 'Wulf' in Woolverstone. Names mentioned on the plates are also included in the index.

Abell, Thomas, 88

Addison, Charles, 16, 17

Ælfric, 39

Alcote, Thomas, 74

Alcote, William, 74

Alcott, William, 27

Allen, family, 16

Allen, David, 17

Allen, John, 29

Ames, family, 80

Andrewes, William, 21, 22, 23, 25, 29, 30, 34, 44, 45

Annyng, Thomas, 28, 44

Appylton, Thomas, Pl. 1

Arnold, family, 43

Arnold, Thomas, 74, 101: n.44

Backlar, Thomas, 74

Bacon, family, 2

Bacon, Philip, 28

Bacon, Robert, 34

Badele, Ralph de, 74

Bakeler, family, 20, 74

Bakeler, John, 30, 31, 33, 42, 74

Bakeler, Richard, 33, 74

Bakeler, Robert, 42, 74, Pl. 1

Bakeler, Thomas, 21, 23, 30, 33, 36, 43, 74

Bakeler, William, 30

Baker, family, 11, 21, 74

Baldwin, family, 21, 74

Barefoot, Peter, 6

Barker, family, 11, 15

Barker, Elizabeth, 36

Barker, Richard, 45

Barker, William, 22

Bataylle, Alice, 36

Bataylle, John, 21, 74

Bataylle, Margaret, 21, 74

Bataylle, Thomas, 36

Bedingfield, family, 2

Berners, family, 29, 31, 33, 38, 85, 93

Berners, Captain Hugh, 4, Pl. 24

Berners, Charles, 2, 3, 12, 21, 23, 32, 35, 42, 45, 57, 58, 70, 76, Pl. 7

Berners, Charles Hugh, 5

Berners, Geoffrey, 3, 17

Berners, Geoffrey Hugh, 2

Berners, John, 3-4

Berners, John Anstruther, 2

Berners, Revd Henry Denny, 11, 35
Berners, Revd Ralph, 11
Berners, William, 2, 3, 21, 22, 23, 23, 27, 34, 36, 41, 43, 46, 59, 69, 70, 71, 84
Bickmore, family, 21, 38, 57
Bickmore, John, 75
Bidwells, agents, 5
Bird, John, 17
Birnes, Cecilia, 45
Blithe, Christine, 75, 101: n.47
Blithes, 76
Boldero, Francis, 75
Boldwennes, 22, 74
Boldwynes, 22, 74
Boone, Charles, 22, 23, 36, 42
Boothman, John, Pl. 1
Bordendale, John de, 75
Bordmales, family, 22
Boreham, Mary, 17
Bowel, Richard, 30
Bowele, Richard, 25
Bowle, Henry, 37, 46
Bowle, Richard, 30
Braham, Hugh de, 36, 75
Braham, John, 75
Brampston, family 75
Brampston, Thomas, 22
Bramston, family, 59, 75-6
Bramston, Charles, 38
Bramston, Lucy, 28
Bramston, Roger, 28
Bramston, Thomas, 20, 24, 25, 28, 33, 35, 36, 75
Bramston, William, 27, 40, 89
Brandeston, Thomas, 24, 75, 84

Brandistone, Roger, 75
Brannston, Thomas, 75, 101: n.49
Bretun, Rannulf, 87
Bridges, family, 23, 76
Brigge, Robert, 76
Briggs, John, 21
Briggs, Robert, 76
Brome, Richard, 24
Brook, Robert, 43
Bruce, Stephen, 35
Bryan, Richard, 44
Brygge, family, 85
Brygges, family, 76
Brygges, Robert, 76, 101: n.50
Brygys, Robert, 76
Bugg, John, 21
Bugge, William, 27
Bunches, Robert, 87
Burcham, John, 25
Burleigh, Barnaby, 22, 44, 46
Busshman, John, 22, 30
Busshman, Robert, 24
Buylin, Matthew de, 77
Buylin, Simon de, 76
Bylam, family, 16, 38, 40
Cages, family, 42, 76
Caketon, Robert, 22, 23-4, 77
Caketon, William de, 77
Candysshe, John, 22, 27, 32, 37, 37, 43, Pl. 2
Candysshe, Thomas, 27, 28, 29, 31, 36, 40, 44
Catchpool, Benjamin, 16
Catelyn, family, 2
Catelyn, Philip, 21, 22, 23, 25, 27, 28, 29, 29, 30, 30, 32, 34, 35, 41, 44, 45, 84

INDEX OF PERSONAL NAMES

Cawell, William, 24

Ceola, 77

Ceolmund, 63, 77

Chapman, John, 20, 44

Chychehaugh, John, 46

Clerk, George, 33

Cobbe, John, 47

Cobbold, John, 17

Cobbold, John Chevallier, 30

Conyers, Thomas, 22

Cook, family, 14, 16, 17

Cook, John, 42

Cook, Margaret, 30

Cooper, family, 35

Cortel, 79

Crack, Cecil, 17

Crane, family, 26, 79

Crane, John, 38

Cukkook, family, 38

Cukhook, John, 22

Cukkok, Thomas, 28

Culpho, John, 21, 22

Culpho, Thomas, 27

Dalton, Timothy, 32, 41, Pl. 14

Dameron, 43

Danske, family, 31

Danske, Francis, 21, 29, 31, 36, 37, 39, 40

Danyell, George, 42

Davy, Henry, 4, Pl. 20

Denic, 79

Dickerson, family, 15

Doneton, Nicolas de, 26, 79

Double, Paul, 13

Driver, John, 34

Driver, Robert, 17

Dunna, 63, 68, 79

Eaton, William, 17

Elderobordes, 80

Elmer, John, 16

Emme, Roger, 80

Emmes, family, 27, 80

Emms, family, 27, 80

Fairbrother, Henry, 23

Farrar, Austin, 6

Fastolf, Katherine, Pl. 2

Felton, John, 20, 44

Felton, Sir Thomas, 29, 43

Felton, Thomas, 34

Ffen, John, 21

Ffuller, Robert, 25

Ffuller, Walter, 30

Ffybet, Richard, 23

Fibet, Richard, 25

Fisk, family, 72

Fisk, Kenneth, 14

Fitch, family, 70

Fitzraffe, Elizabeth, 2

Fletcher, family, 28

Flecher, Thomas, 80

Frost, William, 37

Fuller, John, 28, 37, Pl. 1

Fuller, Robert, 29

Fuller, Roger, 22

Gardiner, John, 43

Gawdy, Henry, 20, 24, 25, 28, 33, 34, 36, 84

Gawdy, Sir Thomas, 2

Gibb, family, 29

Gibbis, family, 81

Gibbs, family, 37

Gibbs, Robert, 16

Gilbert, Earl, 88

Giles, Robert, 32

Gippa, 81
Glandfield, Benjamin, 29
Glanfield, Robert, 27
Godefroy, Andrew, 81
Godfrey, family, 29, 81, 87
Godman, family, 81
Goldson, family, 45
Goldson, John, 33, 43
Goldstone, John, 38
Goodyng, Thomas, 44
Goose, Robert, 17
Gouldson, John, 33, 38, 45
Grace, 29
Green, family, 15, 16
Greenleffe, John, 46
Greneleffe, John, 46
Grimwood, Mary, 17
Hamblin, family, 38
Harre, William, 82
Hayle, 24
Hayward, Christopher, 32, 41
Head, William, 17
Hell, John att, 26
Herre, William, 82
Hervey, Elizabeth, 39
Hervey, Simon, 39
Heth, John, 33
Hetham, John, 26, 30, 36
Hetham, Philip, 27
Hetham, Rose, 26
Hewarde, Robert, 23
Heyward, Thomas, 35
Heywarde, Robert, 76
Hill, George, 16
Hill, Vic, 12, 72
Hob, 82
Hodskinson, family, 69, Pl. 5

Holton, family, 15
Igram, Rose, 41
Ingram, Richard, 32, 41
Ingram, Rose, 21, 32, 43
Ingram, Thomas, 24
Jirnetts, family, 83
Johnson, Charles, 16
Johnson, John, 3, 99: n.11
Jones, family, 67
Jones, John, 83
Juferby, Thomas, 21, 26, 29, 31
Ketill, 83
Kettle, 83
Ketyl, 83
Klopfer, 14
Knapp, family, 43
Knapp, Edmond, 26, 45
Knapp, Edmund, 44
Knapp, Elizabeth, 44
Knappe, Edmund, 22
Lambard, family, 28, 33, 83, 90
Lambert, family, 90
Langheth, John (?), Pl. 1
Latymer, Edward, 21, 23, 28, 30,
    31, 33, 36, 37, 42, 43, 45
Leggatt, family, 15
Leggatt, John, 14, 17, 101: n.43
Lopham, family, 70, 84
Lopham, Roger de, 84
Lopham, William de, 70
Loppa, 84
Lord, Hugh, 26, 46
Lucas, family, 12
Lucas, John, 39
Lucas, Mary, 39
Lucas, Mary, 40

Lucas, Samuel, 20, 21, 29, 30, 31, 32, 33, 34, 38, 40, 42, 45, 46

Lucas, Susan, 17

Lutyens, Edwin, 5, 13, Pls. 21 & 22

Mabbes, family, 34

Mabesyn, Richard, 25

Mabysyn, Thomas, 84

Mann, John, 40

Manning, family, 17, 60

Marcham, family, 84

Marchamt, family, 84

Marston, family, 11, 16

Mary, 34, 35, 59, 84

Mason, family, 11, 15, 45

Matthews, Thomas, 12

Meadowes, Robert, 41

Mellsupp, William, 34

Mills, Robert, 16

Morman, family, 85

Mowslowe, 59, 66, 76

Muddyclift, Ann, 33

Munnings, Robert, 21, 29, 31, 37, 39, 40

Mylne, Robert, 99: n.12

Mynt, James, 34, 37

Nelson, family, Pl. 14

Neweman, John, 20, Pl. 1

Neweman, William, Pl. 1

Newham, Christopher, 20, 21, 29, 30, 31, 32, 33, 34, 40, 42, 45, 46

Newman, John, 61, 64

Orger, Thomas, 70

Osbern, 39-40, 88

Page, family, 59, 66, 67

Pain(e), family, 35

Paine, Elizabeth, 35

Parker, family, 2, 15, 30, 33, 41

Parker, Sir Calthorp, 24

Peck, family, 29

Peckman, William, 40

Pecks, family, 81

Pekesome, John, Pl. 1

Perye, Roger atte, 25

Pesehelles, family, 87

Pesel, William, 87

Pesell, family, 87

Peselys, family, 87

Petman, family, 43, 68

Petman, Thomas, 43, Pl. 4

Pett, family, 22

Pett, Henry, 35, 44, 87

Pett, John, 87

Pett, John att, 87

Pick, family, 87

Picksomes, 39

Picksomers, 39

Pitman, Thomas, 32, 43

Pod, Agnes, 30, 35, 87

Pod, Laurence, 30, 35, 87

Podd, John, 16

Podds, family, 87

Pollard, Abraham, 12

Pompard, family, 87

Pondere, Ada, 27

Potts, family, 87

Pourtepet, William de, 88

Pratt, family, 13

Prekyll, John, the elder, Pl. 4

Prekytt, John, 43

Prinny, family, 88

Purpet, Thomas, 40

Purtepet, Walter, 40, 88

Pyckesomyr, William, 87
Pyk, Richard, 86, 87
Pykesome, John, 21
Pyksomes, John, 87
Pylburgh, James, 39
Pyllion, Richard, 75
Quinn, 89
Raimes, Gilbert de, 36
Read, Walter, Pl. 1
Read, William, Pl. 1
Rede, John, 42
Rede, Simon de, 89
Reed, Walter, 89
Reed, Willian, 89
Reeve, Samuel, 16
Reynolds, Sarah, 33
Richard, son of Earl Gilbert, 88
Richardson, family, 59, 76, 85,
    Pls. 11, 12, 13
Robert, 82
Roberts, 'Old', 79
Robin, family, 82
Robyn, family, 89
Rolfe, family, 42
Rolfe, Christopher, 30
Rolfe, Stephen, 45
Rosier, Jonathon, 29
Rous, family, 2
Rouse, family, 35
Rudland, family, 20
Runting, family, 89
Runtyng, family, 89
Runtyng, Nicholas, 21
Runtyng, Simon, 89
Runtyng, Thomas, 89
Rybely, John, 21
Sage, family, 18

Sage, Joseph, 35
Sampson, family, 21
Sampson, Thomas, 26
Sargeant, family, 89
Sargent, John, 35, 41, 89
Sarjeant, family, 46
Sarjent, family, 89
Scarfe, family, 11, 15
Scarfe, John, 16
Scott, Sir Giles Gilbert, 4
Sebbyng, family, 89
Sewell, James, 23
Sherman, Robert, 23, 30, 35, 43
Sholande, Matilda de, 42, 90
Smith, family, 30
Smyth, John, 24, 39
Smyth, Margaret, 38, 39
Smyth, Roger, 31
Smyth, William, 24
Smythe, John, 38
Snell, Edward, 23
Snell, John, 23, 45
Snell, Nicholas, 27, 39, 45
Snell, Richard, 23, 24, 32, 45
Snell, Thomas, 20, 25, 43
Sparrowe, Robert, 40
Spetman, family, 28, 33, 83, 90
Spetman, Thomas, 90
Spurling, John, 11
St Aubyn, architect, 4
Stisted, Robert, 43
Stisted, Thomas, 21, 29, 31, 37,
    39, 40
Stratton, John, Pl. 1
Strowle, John, 81
Stuart, Samuel, 17
Stutton, family, 90

Sukkook, Phillip, 38
Tendering, William, 101: n.63
Tenderyng, Elizabeth, Pl. 2
Tenderyng, William, 40, 88
Thurston, Thomas, 37, 46
Tracey, family, 29, 90
Tracey, Robert, 43, 59, 90
Trueford, family, 90
Tusser, Thomas, 75
Tyler, family, 22, 91
Tyssen, John, 2, 32, 34, 69
Wade, William, 28
Wadling, architect, 4
Walton, Thomas, 44
Warbilton, Thomas, 91
Warburton, John, 31, 44, 91
Warbylton, family, 91
Ward, John, 2, 34
Ward, Knox, 2, 46, 59, 69
Ward, Ralph, 46
Warren, William, 17
Warrey, John, 81
Warry, George, 45, 92
Warrye, George, 92
Webb, Thomas, 17
Webster, Jeremiah, 16
Wells, John, 39
White, family, 72

Whitehouse, Jack, 5
Whytyng, family, 42, 46
Whytyng, John, 46, 92, 93
Winney, William, 17
Wolferston / Wolfreston /
    Wulferston / Wolverston,
    family, 46, 93
Wolferston, Alice, 65
Wolferston / Wolverston /
    Wulferston, Elizabeth [de],
    1, 21, 24, 27, 31, 41, 42, 75,
    77, 78, 84, 99: n.5
Wolferston / Wolverston, Philip
    de, 2
Wolferston / Wolverston,
    Richard, 24, 28, 77
Wolferston / Wolverston, Robert,
    5
Wolferston / Wolfreston /
    Wolverston, Roger [de], 2,
    26, 65
Wolferston / Wolverston /
    Wulferston, Thomas de, 2, 75
Wolfreston, Thomas, Pl. 3
Wulf, eponymous founder, 1, 83,
    93
Wulfere, 83
Wulfhere, 63, 64
Wyles, John, 38

SUBSCRIBERS

The publisher and author are extremely grateful to the following subscribers (in alphabetical order) who made this book possible:

Miss G. M. Abbott, Chelmondiston
Mrs J. E. Abbott, Harkstead
J. L. Allgrove, Poole
Mrs G. M. Ardern, Harkstead
Gerald & Ursula Askew, Freston
Jean Austin, Ipswich
Miss C. Baron, Cheltenham
Mrs P. B. Bird, Brantham
J. M. Bowers, Sweffling
Mrs June Brereton, Bramfield
Lord Bridges, Orford
Sheila Brooks, Redgrave
Mrs Sylvia Caldwell-Smith, Flowton
A. L. P. Carter, Toft
Marjorie Carter, Chelmondiston
Dr & Mrs M. Channon, Eye
P. Christie, Bideford
Miss G. E. Churley, Woolverstone
Mrs E. D. Claydon, Chilbolton
Mrs J. M. Clement, Woodbridge
Mrs Hilary Clutten, Pulham St Mary
Patrick J. Corness, Coventry
A. W. Cowley, Chelmondiston
J. Cowley, London (2 copies)
Mrs V. E. Crack, Chelmondiston
Judy Cracknell, Woolverstone
Dr B. E. Crawford, St Andrews
Lionel & Elizabeth Crawford, Shotley
Wendy Crease, Hitcham
M. S. Crellin, Woodbridge
Miss E. H. Cuthbert, Harlow
Richard D. Davies, Leeds
D. C. Davis, Cheadle
Mrs Norma Dawlings, Northwood (2 copies)
B. Deane, Freston Hill
Deben Valley Placename Survey, Woodbridge

SUBSCRIBERS

Professor Klaus Dietz, Berlin, Germany
Jean Double, Woolverstone
Mrs J. D. Double, Woolverstone
Mrs E. V. Downing, Cheltenham
Wilfred T. Edwards, London
Mrs E. H. Elbourne, Needham Market
Mrs M. Elliott, Charsfield
Glyn Evans, Holbrook
John Fairclough, Ipswich
G. Farthing, Ipswich
Gillian Fellows-Jensen, Karlslunde, Denmark
Trevor Foulds, Nottingham
Mrs Ida Fryer, Stutton
A. E. Gibbons, London
Peter, Allison, Benjamin & Abigail Glading, Woolverstone
T. Gondris, Ipswich
Mrs Margaret Gooch, Woolverstone
David Gould, Stroud
Michael Graves, Ipswich
Mrs G. M. Gray, Ipswich
Mrs G. Hall, Capel St Mary
M. J. Hardy, Wortwell
Professor C. Harper-Bill, Twickenham
Dr D. J. Harris, Lee on the Solent
Martin Harrison, Pakenham
Colin J. Hawes, Bentley
John Hayward, London
Mrs D. C. Heath, Walsall
Mrs S. Herring, Needham Market
S. J. Hines, Ipswich
L. L. Holland, Holbrook
Desmond Hollox, Calgary, Canada
Carole Hough, Chaddesden
Brenda Hudson, Coddenham
Gillian Hutchings, Freston
Miss G. J. Hutchinson, Luton
Enid Hyde, Woolverstone
Ipswich Institute Library, Ipswich
Mrs A. H. Jarvis, Felixstowe
Mrs G. M. Jillings, Chelmondiston
Valerie Johnston, Kirkmichael
P. S. Keate, Cradley Heath
Mrs J. F. Keeble, Manningtree

J. A. Kendrick, Woolverstone
Mrs P. H. Kent, Holbrook (3 copies)
Miss J. A. Kimber, Netley Abbey
Mrs R. Knox, Nayland
Kobenhavns Universitet, Copenhagen, Denmark
Mrs Sally Laws, Holbrook
Derek Lay, Barham
Eleanor Leigh, Bentley
Martin Lewis, Woolverstone
Margaret Lichtenhein, Woolverstone
Mrs J. Lindsay, Curtin, Australia
Mrs Judith Longman, Lower Holbrook
Mrs Rosalind Lowe, Goodrich
Dr Alan Mackley, Blythburgh
Brian Mann, Chelmondiston
Edward Martin, Hitcham
Miss C. Mason, Dovercourt
S. D. Mattock, Harrogate
Mrs H. A. Maudsley, Capel St Mary
Mr & Mrs A. W. Mayhew, Chelmondiston
Mrs I. McMaster, Mount Bures
Joan Melville-Jackson, Kirton
Mrs N. Monckton, Fettercairn, Scotland
Mrs S. M. Mower, Shotley
K. & J. Nixon, Chelmondiston
Barbara Norman, Woolverstone (2 copies)
Joy O'Keefe, Ringwood
R. Paine, Harkstead
C. J. Pankhurst, Ipswich
Mrs A. Parry, Shotley Gate
Mrs J. M. Paul, Freston
Ian Philion, London
Mrs D. H. Pickford, Canons Town
Richard Pipe, Washbrook
W. P. Platt, Stambourne
Fay & Michael Poole, Woolverstone
Andrew J. Pye, Steeple Morden
Mrs E. Pyefinch, Pitlochry, Scotland
R. Rands, Woodmancote
S. Rayson, Harkstead
Dr Arthur Richmond, Guisborough
Simon Roberts, Halesworth
Adrian Room, Stamford

SUBSCRIBERS

Dr D. F. Sanders, Horney
Norman Scarfe, Woodbridge
Jennifer Scherr, Bristol
V. Scott, Stutton
J. W. Searle, Abbots Manor
Mrs Phyllis Sharman, Woolverstone
Mrs Vivien Shiells, Farnham
Mrs R. P. J. Ship, Woolverstone
Dr. P. D. Simmons, London
Mrs B. I. Sims, Bramford
Mrs M. Spencer, Capel St Mary
C. M. Spurling, Bury St Edmunds
C. F. Stephenson, Middleton
Stutton Local History Group, Stutton
Suffolk Record Office, Ipswich
K. S. Sunaway, Woodbridge
D. A. Taylor, Wherstead
Michael Taylor, Thelwall
Mrs H. Thomas, Woolverstone
D. R. W. Thornbery, Chelmondiston
J. N. W. Tripp, Norwich
Naoki Tsukada, Saitama, Japan
Jean Tsushima, Great Bedwyn
Mrs Turville-Petre, Aylsham
Ian D. Tyas, Saltburn-by-the-Sea
Professor K. Ugawa, Tokyo, Japan
C. & L. Underwood, Glasgow
Eleanor Vollans, Oakham
E. J. Wagstaff, Felixstowe
Renee M. Waite, Ipswich
Dr D. J. C. Walker, Harkstead
Gordon A. Watts, Harkstead
Ronald Webb, Galashiels
Mrs Denise Welford, Stratford St Mary
John Weller, Bildeston
Karin Wheals, Bentley
Jack Whitehead, London
Alan Whyard, Felixstowe
Mrs B. M. Wilkinson, Badingham
Mrs Greta Williams, Holbrook
Philip W. Willis, Stutton
M. L. Winney, Congleton
W. M. Winter, London

Mr & Mrs L. Woolford, Woolverstone (4 copies)
David Wordley, Norton
J. E. Wrinch, Chelmondiston
Peter S. Wyant, Regina, Canada
Mr & Mrs D. H. Yelland, Woolverstone
Mrs M. L. Young, Harkstead

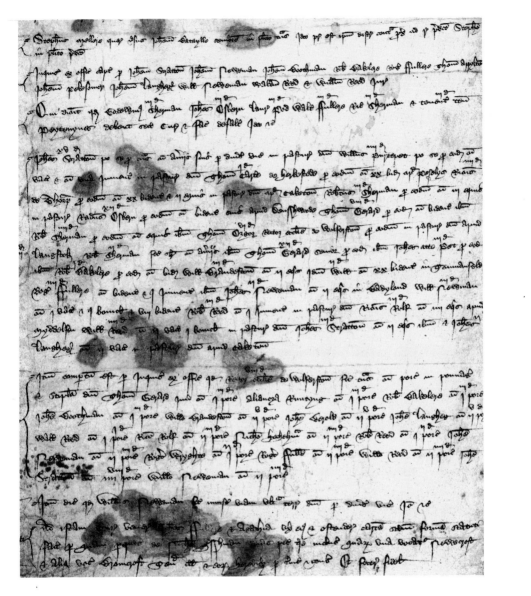

Plate 1: Extract from the earliest surviving court roll of Wolverston Manor, 1348.
The jurors were John Stratton, John Neweman, John Boothman, Robert Bakeler,
John Fuller, Thomas Appylton, John Pekesome, John (?) Langheth, William
Neweman, Walter Read and William Read.

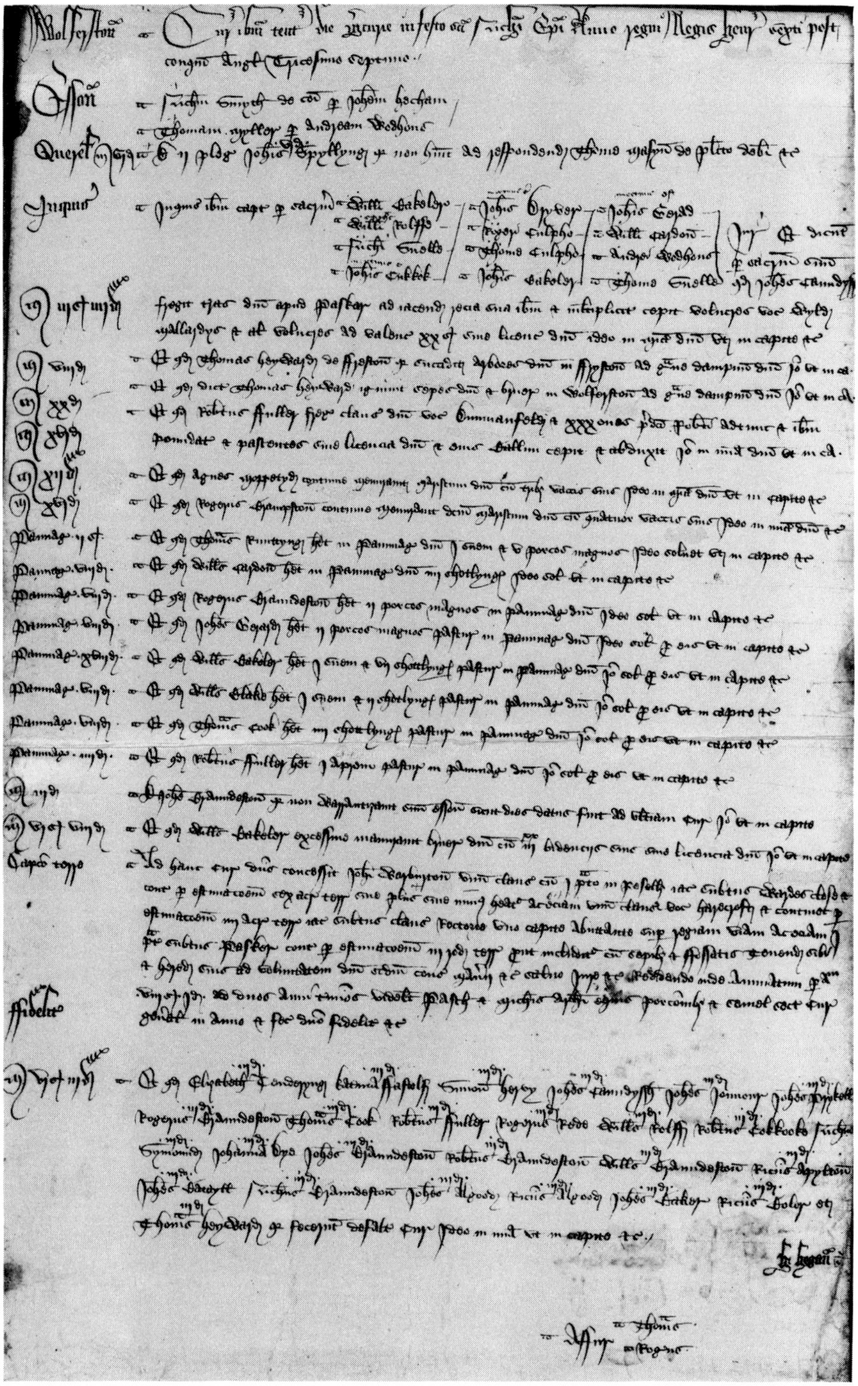

Plate 2: Extract from the court roll of 1459. John Candysshe was amerced for netting wild mallards at *Pasker*. Twenty-five people were in default, owing suit of court, including Elizabeth Tenderyng and Katherine Fastolf.

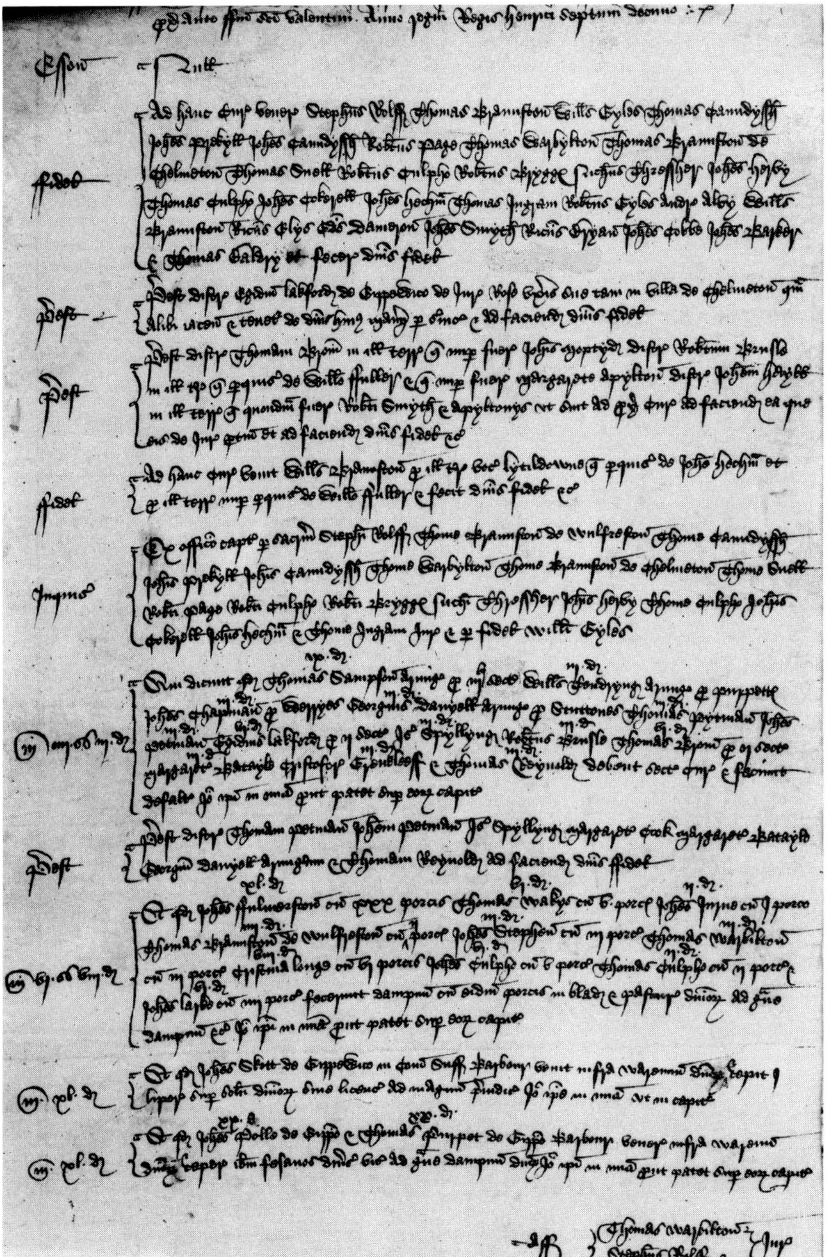

Plate 3: At the first court of Thomas Wolfreston (1495), held on the Thursday next before the Feast of St Valentine, twenty-eight men took the oath of fealty.

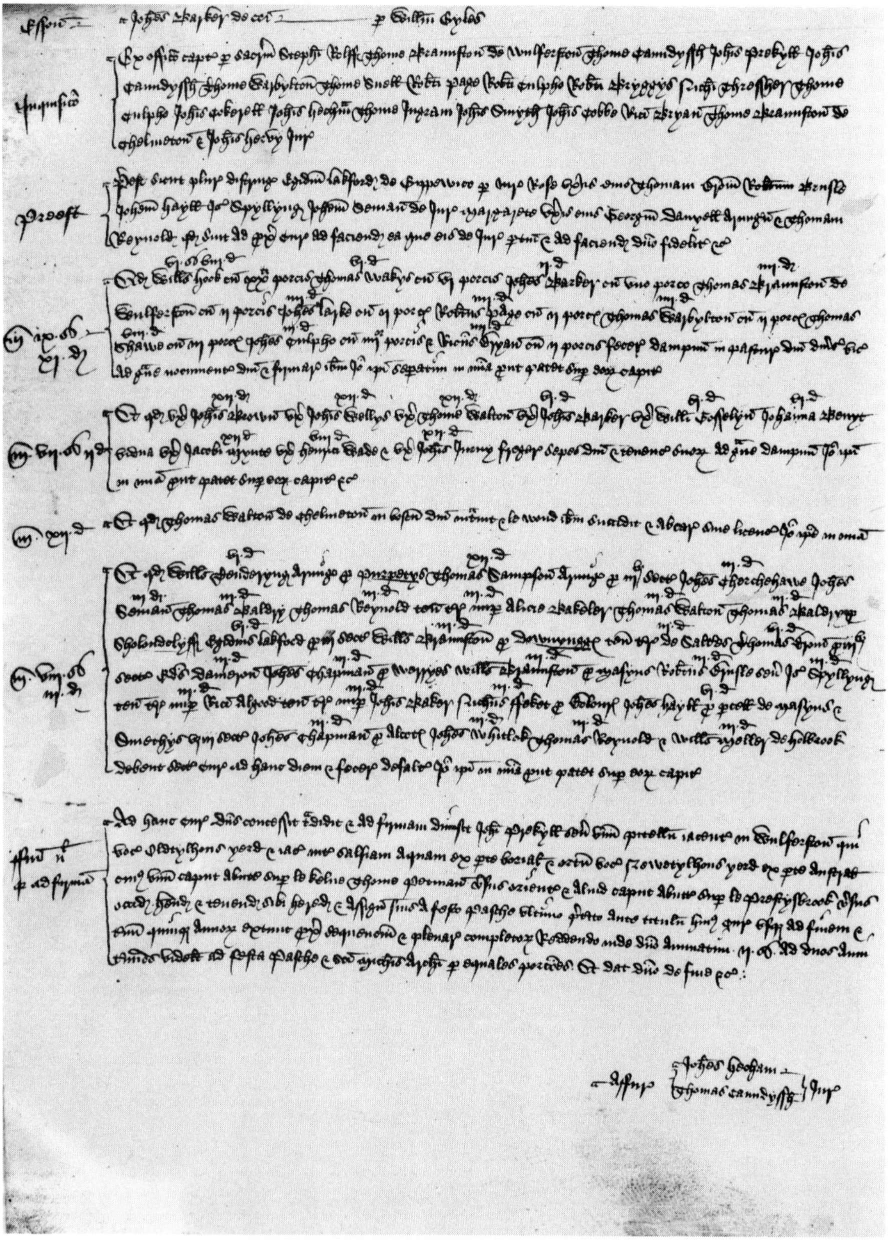

Plate 4: This extract from the 1497 court roll records a five-year lease of the *Oldtylhousyerd* (between the Salt Water and the *Newtylhousyerd*) to John Prekyll the elder; *le Kelne* of Thomas Petman lay towards the east

Plate 5: detail from Hodskinson's map of 1783 showing the extent of Woolverstone Park on the Shotley Peninsula. The village is already well established outside William Berners' new park

Plate 6 (a) (above): map showing the extent of the Woolverstone Hall Estate in 1937, as published in the sales particulars

Plate 6 (b) (left): The plan of the same estate as published in *The Times* (2 December 1937)

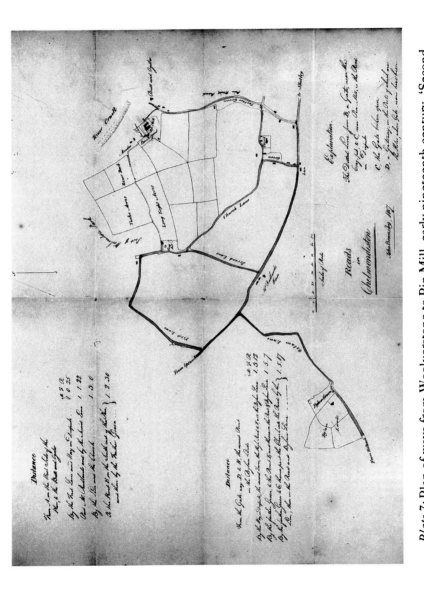

Plate 7: Plan of ways from Woolverstone to Pin Mill, early nineteenth century. 'Second Lane' continued to Pin Mill until closed by Charles Berners; it is still a public path

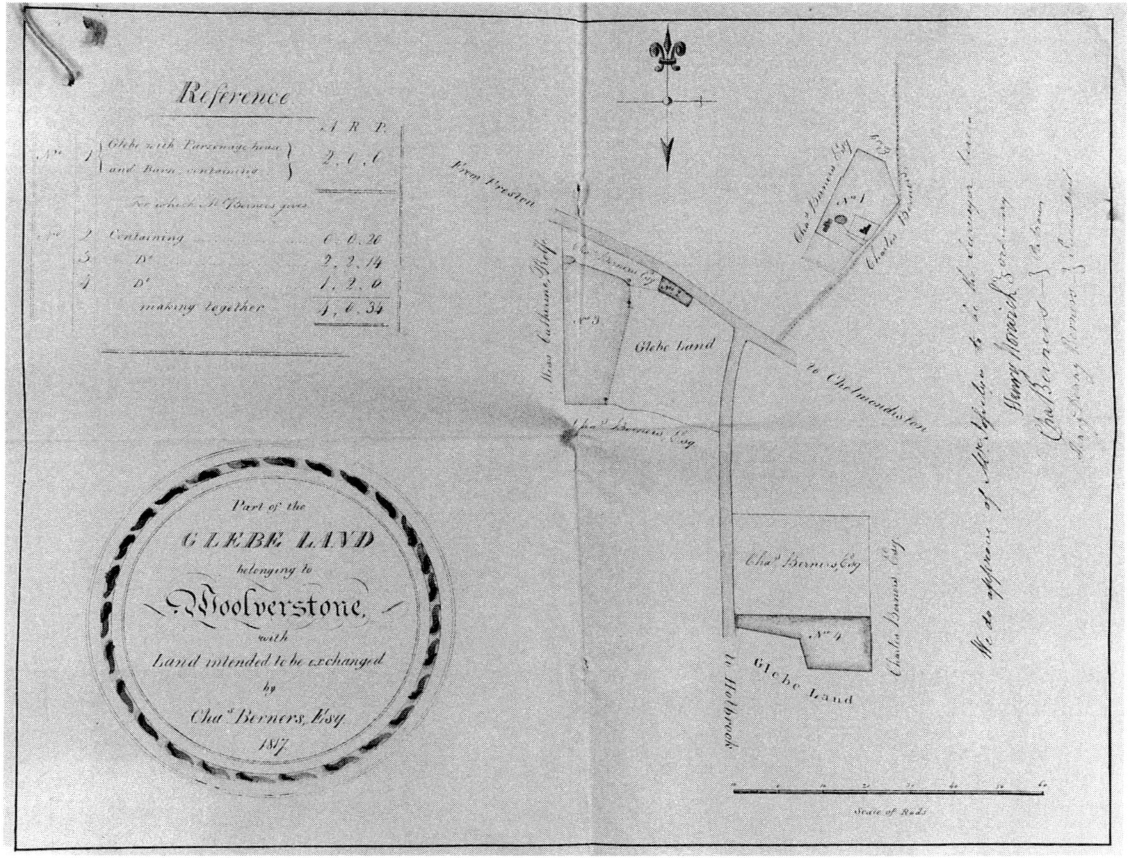

Plate 8: Plan of Woolverstone rectory and glebe land (1817) before the building was demolished and the land emparked

Plate 9: Aerial photograph of West Field, Sandpit Field and Whinney Field, Woolverstone, with crop marks that may indicate the margins of an early settlement. Woolverstone Home Farm appears top centre with Mannings Lane left

Plate 10: This Chelmondiston field borders the Ipswich-Shotley road (bottom of picture). The crop marks, clearly visible from the air in the 1975 drought, indicate field systems of unknown date. Field work suggests that the area has been occupied and farmed for at least 2,000 years

Plate 11: Aerial photograph of Woolverstone taken in 1994

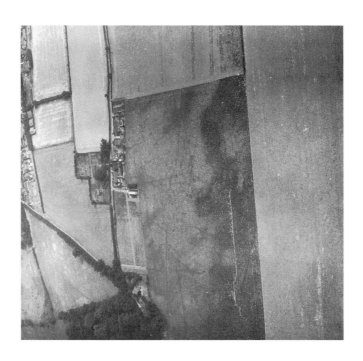

Plate 14 (above): Corner Field, Woolverstone, opposite Nelson's Avenue, was called Shambles in the seventeenth century. The crop marks may relate to the mansion built there by the Revd Timothy Dalton, Puritan rector of Woolverstone

Plates 12 and 13 (opposite): These aerial photographs provide closer views of the field shown in plate 10, concentrating on the Richardson's Lane area.

Plate 15: Enigmatic crop-marks in Park Field, Woolverstone, appear between the drive to Woolverstone Marina and the curving line of the nineteenth-century carriage drive

Plate 16: Lower Park Field, Woolverstone. The two round clumps of trees
(shown lower right in this aerial photograph) may mask Bronze Age burial mounds

Plate 17: A 1971 aerial survey photograph shows small fields still existing in Woolverstone at that time

Plate 18: A medieval tile kiln exposed by erosion of the Orwell river bank in 1991

Plate 19: A pencil sketch of the Old Manor House, Woolverstone, *c.*1776.
Behind a brick façade was a timber-framed building with two chambers over
the hall, a cellar beneath and a 'kitching'

Plate 20: Church of St Michael the Archangel, Woolverstone. Engraving by H. Davy, made in 1838 before major alterations

Plate 21: Sisters of St Peter's Community sheltering beside the chapel at St Peter's Home, Woolverstone. The architect was Edwin Lutyens

Plate 22: Their chapel, long since demolished, which at one time was used as a dormitory for the boys of Woolverstone Hall School

WOLVERSTONE PARK, SUFFOLK.
The Seat of Charles Berners, Esq.

Plate 23: An early nineteenth-century engraving of Woolverstone Park and the Cat House

Plate 24: The Widows' Homes, Woolverstone, a block of six cottages built for Captain Hugh Berners in 1877